Placing the Social Economy

In recent years there has been a great deal of talk about the social economy and its role in a new 'Third Way', a term that has attained a level of household recognition, especially in North America and Britain. Academics and commentators have debated the potential of the social economy as a restraint on capitalist excesses with critics arguing that it is but a poor substitute for the welfare state. This book provides a refreshing and accessible account of real life experience in a social economy.

By focusing on new evidence, this book critically analyses such themes as:

- the range of academic and policy expectations that have emerged in recent years in the developed world
- the policies of New Labour in Britain
- the dynamics of social enterprises in Bristol, London, Middlesbrough, and Glasgow.

These critical assessments lead the authors to reflect on the future of the social economy and the policy changes that could potentially maximise whatever opportunity the sector provides.

This book's evidence-based approach will make it popular with academics interested in the fields of welfare, and social and political economics. Its easy-to-follow, accessible style will provide students in these areas with an important source for understanding contemporary economies, while its recommendations should be required reading for public policy makers and advisors.

Ash Amin is Professor of Geography at the University of Durham. **Angus Cameron** is lecturer in the Department of Geography at the University of Leicester. **Ray Hudson** is Professor of Geography at the University of Durham and Chairman of the International Centre for Regional Regeneration and Development Studies.

Contemporary Political Economy series
Edited by Jonathan Michie
Birkbeck College, University of London, UK

This series presents a fresh, broad perspective on the key issues in the modern world economy, drawing in perspectives from management and business, politics and sociology, economic history and law.

Written in a lively and accessible style, it will present focused and comprehensive introductions to key topics, demonstrating the relevance of political economy to major debates in economics and to an understanding of the contemporary world.

Global Instability
The political economy of world economic governance
Edited by Jonathan Michie and John Grieve Smith

Reconstructing Political Economy
The great divide in economic thought
William K. Tabb

The Political Economy of Competitiveness
Employment, public policy and corporate performance
Michael Kitson and Jonathan Michie

Global Economy, Global Justice
Theoretical objections and policy alternatives to neoliberalism
George F. DeMartino

Social Capital Versus Social Theory
Political economy and social science at the turn of the millennium
Ben Fine

A New Guide to Post Keynesian Economics
Steven Pressman and Richard Holt

Placing the Social Economy
Ash Amin, Angus Cameron and Ray Hudson

Placing the Social Economy

Ash Amin, Angus Cameron and Ray Hudson

London and New York

First published 2002
by Routledge
11 New Fetter Lane, London EC4P 4EE

Simultaneously published in the USA and Canada
by Routledge
29 West 35th Street, New York, NY 10001

Routledge is an imprint of the Taylor & Francis Group

© 2002 Ash Amin, Angus Cameron and Ray Hudson

Typeset in Galliard by
BOOK NOW Ltd
Printed and bound in Great Britain by
TJ International Ltd, Padstow, Cornwall

1006191775

British Library Cataloguing in Publication Data
A catalogue record for this book is available from the British Library

Library of Congress Cataloging in Publication Data
A record for this book has been requested

ISBN 0-415-26088-4 (hbk)
ISBN 0-415-26089-2 (pbk)

Contents

Illustrations

Plates

Figures

Tables

Preface

There is a great deal of talk these days about the restorative powers of the social economy. The non-profit sector, usually in the hands of the Third Sector, is no longer seen as a residual and poor cousin to the state or the market, a sphere of charity and social or moral repair. Instead, it is imagined as a mainstay of future social organisation in both the developed and developing world, set to co-exist with the welfare state, meet social needs in hard-pressed communities, constitute a new economic circuit of jobs and enterprises in a market composed of socially useful goods and services, empower the socially excluded by combining training and skills formation with capacity and confidence-building, and create a space for humane, co-operative, sustainable, and 'alternative' forms of social and economic organisation. While the optimists have come to see much of this as a good thing, a 'taming' of capitalist excess and exploitation, and the return of the social and civic into the mainstream, those who are more circumspect warn that the social economy remains a poor substitute for provision through the market or welfare state, the return of an under-nourished and under-nourishing social sphere. Either way, there is a distinct sense that the social economy will feature centrally in twenty-first century capitalism.

The social economy, as defined by this book, consists of non-profit activities designed to combat social exclusion through socially useful goods sold in the market and which are not provided for by the state or the private sector. The social economy generates jobs and entrepreneurship by meeting social needs and very often by deploying the socially excluded.

This book provides a sober, evidence-based, account of experience in the social economy, in order to evaluate its strengths and weaknesses, and its future potential. We examine and explain the range of expectations – academic and policy – that have emerged in recent years across the developed world (Chapters 1 and 2). We then focus on the policies of New Labour in Britain – increasingly presented as a paradigmatic 'Third Way' that typifies the new centrality of the social economy – and evaluate their expectations against experience on the ground in the UK (Chapter 3). As much of the contemporary rhetoric surrounding the social economy is based around the powers of place, in essence the argument that local community mobilisation for local provision can help resolve local social exclusion, Chapters 4 and 5 compare the dynamics of social enterprises in four urban areas – Bristol, Tower Hamlets in London, Middlesbrough, and Glasgow. These case studies illustrate the marked variety in form and experience that we find between places and explore the ways in which local context matters. The final chapter uses the evidence to reflect on the future potential of the social economy and ends with a series of policy recommendations to maximise whatever potential the sector provides.

The evidence is based on two large-scale research projects we carried out between 1997–2001 into the practices and experiences of social economy organisations in the UK. The first of these, commissioned by European Commission, sampled nearly 2000 Third Sector initiatives, to select sixty examples of 'best practice' for inclusion in the Commission's multi-country database of over 700 projects labelled 'Local Initiatives to Combat Social Exclusion in Europe' (LOCIN).[1] Although the LOCIN project was successful in its own terms, from our perspective, like so many other similar approaches, it also highlighted some of the limitations of 'best practice' approaches to the social economy. Specifically, we felt that in only examining projects that were 'successful', such studies did not question how success was measured, failed to explain success, eliminated the specificity of place from the analysis, and glossed over the very high rates of failure amongst social economy organisations.

To investigate these wider questions a further project was commenced in 1999, funded by the UK's Economic and Social Research Council (R000 23 7967), which undertook a more critical and place-based analysis of UK social economy practice. Rather than investigating isolated examples of best practice, the second study sought to examine the dynamics of success and failure in different types of social enterprise and in different local settings. We selected the above four areas because all were known (or at least reputed) to have some degree of social economy activity in existence, having experienced significant problems of poverty and social exclusion, but also because all four have widely differing social, civic, political and economic conditions; differences that might explain the variety. The issue of success and failure was, from the outset, treated as problematic and one not amenable to being reduced to the simple, usually quantitative, metrics often used to gauge the relative value of social economy organisations. Hence the possibility was raised that some projects could, within their local contexts, be successful in terms of meeting specific local needs but unsuccessful in terms of quantifiable outputs, such as the number of jobs generated. The evidence base of each case study was background secondary material, printed case material, and interviews with forty organisations. The combined database from which the various examples used here are drawn consists of 195 individual social economy projects from throughout the UK. A full list of these projects can be found in the Appendix (p. 126).

What, then, are our main findings? First, we can conclude that there is no such thing as a model social enterprise or model of best practice that can be transplanted and encouraged through standardised policy interventions. What counts as success varies enormously between initiatives, with targets such as building client-confidence and increasing participation often at odds with national policy expectations measured in terms of specific quantifiable outcomes relating to jobs and training, medium to long-term financial sustainability and, less precisely, local economic 'regeneration'. Similarly, our evidence suggests that place and 'local' context are of importance in determining the nature and 'success' of social economy initiatives. For example, the supportive role of the local authority in Glasgow within a specific Labourist political culture has had significant effects on the form that the social economy has taken there, and upon its 'success', while in a similar industrial and social setting such as Middlesbrough, a different state prac-tice has resulted in a much more modest social economy. In contrast, in Bristol a long history of voluntary sector activity, community activism, civic engagement and alternative lifestyles has helped underpin a vibrant social economy. In short, 'success' is a product of a range of place-specific factors that cannot be assumed to exist or be induced elsewhere.

Second, our findings demonstrate that the social economy cannot be concep-tualised without reference to the state or the mainstream economy. It remains generally highly dependent upon the state. Although there are examples of projects that have successfully developed independently of public funds, the majority of social enterprises (even well-known success cases) rely heavily on grant income and/or service level contracts with public authorities. The idea that social enterprises should be able to trade their way out of state dependency, whilst commonplace, does not tally with the experience of existing projects in the UK. The alternative that the social economy offers with respect to the public sector, therefore, is less one of providing a different way of generating resources than a different way of using and distributing them. The relationship between the social economy and the mainstream private sector is also significant, albeit precarious and uneven. In places where the private sector economy is strong, such as in London and Bristol, the social economy has been able to derive considerable benefits. These include the recruitment of staff from local firms, the acquisition of materials and financial donations, and the capacity of local labour markets to absorb trainees coming through the social economy. Where the private sector economy is much weaker, such links cannot develop because there is insufficient density of private sector firms to provide the aggregate level of support.

Third, therefore, we find, against dominant communitarian and Third Way thought, that rarely is the social economy genuinely rooted in the resources of local communities. Indeed, areas of marked social exclusion are precisely those that lack the composite skills and resources necessary to sustain a vibrant social economy, resulting in either highly precarious and short-lived ventures that fail to meet local needs, or ventures reliant upon public sector leadership, peripatetic professionals and social entrepreneurs, dedicated organisations such as religious or minority ethnic bodies, or market links that stretch well beyond the modest offerings available locally. Participation by the local community, when we find it, seems to depend upon two factors: first, the nature of the local community itself (e.g. whether cohesive, self-identifying, active); and second, the way in which the social enterprises engage with local people (e.g. genuine and persistent commit-ment to empowerment and involvement).

Fourth, our evidence shows that it is naïve and unreasonable to expect, as does UK, and increasingly EU, policy and increasingly also EU thinking, that the social economy can be a major source of jobs, entrepreneurship, local regeneration, and welfare provision. To do so, runs the risk of marked disappointment, a return to the vagaries of 'good acts' and 'good people' in combating social exclusion and meeting welfare needs, while legitimating cuts in state expenditure or state welfare remit. We find, instead, that social enterprises – in the right places and with the relevant support – have a role to play that is complementary to provision via state and market. As such, they can achieve something genuinely different. The more successful social enterprises analysed in our research are those that open up new possibilities and networks for people who had previously been confined to the limited resources of poor places. This is not simply a question of altering poor people in poor places to be more like the rest of the 'socially included' world, but a question of opening up and sustaining new ways of being; creating new forms of fulfilling, participatory and democratised work, providing socially useful goods and services, or practising ethical and ecological values. Such an alternative role for the social economy can potentially also influence organisation in the main-stream. This is most obvious when the social economy provides targeted services in a non-bureaucratic and 'hands on' way, or when projects have been able to alter political relationships within local communities – creating new forms of democratic participation as well as economic opportunity.

Finally, therefore, our perspective is at odds with Third Way/New Labour thinking, which charges social enterprises with creating jobs, tackling social exclusion in the round, providing training, developing local services and local markets, and generally countering the effects of years of disinvestment and disengagement by public and private sectors alike. Furthermore, they are expected to become financially viable. Our findings demonstrate quite clearly that the social economy as it is currently constituted cannot deliver this range of outcomes. This is not only because of its own inherent limitations, but because of the different capacities of people and places to develop social economy activities – the poorest places having the least chance of doing so – and because these many problems cannot be tackled solely at the level of local communities. These are multi-scalar problems that demand multi-scalar solutions. The last chapter outlines a series of policy reforms to strengthen the social economy as a complementary, but alternative, sector to state and market, rather than as a substitute for either. Thus, we recommend that, alongside high-quality universal welfare and active state-led regeneration strategies, in the short-to-medium term, there is a need for policies that will encourage innovation, risk-taking in pursuit of social goals, and social entrepreneurial imagination. In the medium-to-longer term we recommend the need to explore alternatives to the conception of the social economy currently dominant in the UK. There is ample evidence that the current Third Way conception can only produce its intended outcomes in quite specific local circumstances – but unfortunately these do no coincide with the places in which the need for alternative forms of provision via the social economy is most acute. There is a serious problem of geographical mismatch, which necessitates an exploration of other conceptions of the social economy, such as those found in continental Europe, which seek to combine a strong commitment to welfare state provision with possibilities also for different forms of local social economy initiatives.

This book is a modest step towards articulating a different vision for the social economy, one that is neither unwarrantedly optimistic, nor unduly pessimistic, and one that accepts the future as both radical change and radical continuity in the relationship between market, state, and society. The book could not have been written as an evidence-based study without the support of the EU's LOCIN programme and the Economic and Social Research Council (ESRC). We thank both organisations. We also wish to thank Robert Langham at Routledge for soliciting this book, and Trudy Graham and David Hume at Durham for helping to put together this book.

Ash Amin, Angus Cameron and Ray Hudson
July 2001

1 The social economy in context

Introduction

In its current usage the term social economy refers to not-for-profit activity geared towards meeting social needs:

> The 'Social Economy' constitutes a broad range of activities which have the potential to provide opportunities for local people and communities to engage in all stages of the process of local economic regeneration and job creation, from the identification of basic needs to the operationalisation of initiatives. The sector covers the economic potential and activities of the self-help and co-operative movements, i.e. initiatives which aim to satisfy social and economic needs of local communities and their members. This sector includes co-operatives; self-help projects; credit unions; housing associations; partnerships; community enterprises and businesses. The Social Economy is the fastest growing sector in Europe and this context is fertile ground for the creation of many new enterprises locally.
>
> (Molloy *et al.* 1999)

Run usually by Third Sector organisations, the social economy covers a range of services, such as training, job and entrepreneurial experience, housing, welfare, consumer services, and environmental upgrading. While organisations may be run as efficient businesses, their prime interest does not lie in profit-maximisation, but in building social capacity (e.g. through employing or training socially disadvantaged groups) and responding to under-met needs (e.g. environmental improvement, free or affordable child-care or housing for low-income families) – and in the process creating new forms of work. The social economy thus marks economic activity (traded and non-traded) with a social remit:

> Social Economy initiatives are based on principles which are concerned primarily with people's needs. Success is judged on the benefits the projects have for the wider community in terms of the number of jobs created; the number of people involved in a voluntary or learning capacity; the benefits to producers and users and in a project's ability to generate income for and within a community. [It] is about effective co-operation, interdependence

and active participation of citizens in the social and economic well-being of local communities. It is concerned with creating an egalitarian, inclusive and more fully democratic society that promotes social justice, fundamental equality, and equality of opportunity.

(Molloy *et al.* 1999)

The aim of this chapter is to explain why interest in the social economy has grown to such a high level of expectation. Until the 1990s, the term hardly featured in English-speaking academic and policy discourse, while older terms such as 'Third Sector', 'non-profit activity', 'community business' or 'voluntary organisation' captured something more modest. They described activity on the margins of a mainstream (non-problematically assumed to be dominated by the state or the private sector) with primarily a welfare function – a safety net or ethical other responding to residual need in a system of provision based on state bureaucracy and market capitalism. They were not seen as part of the economy (as they were not motivated by job generation, entrepreneurship, meeting consumer demand, or producing profit), nor were they seen as political (promoting citizenship, or empowerment). Their role was to see to the welfare of the marginalised. Now, in contrast, much more is expected from the social economy, as we shall see. The chapter begins by tracing the rise of the contemporary discourse on the social economy. It then explores its varied policy interpretations in different national contexts, and ends with a summary of the critical and positive academic interpretations of the potential of the social economy.

From the end of full employment to the crisis of the welfare state

Let us begin with a stylised caricature of the form of capitalist organisation that dominated until recently. Fordism is the term that describes the model of capitalist accumulation and regulation from the mid 1950s to the late 1970s. In its heartland in North America and parts of Europe, during its golden age, it provided full employment, consumer and welfare security, and a social pact around national mass political institutions and universalist beliefs. Its economic logic lay in the employment of large workforces to mass produce goods for a mass consumer market sustained by growing wages, state demand management policies and state welfare provision. A distinctive combination of state and market – centred around the economics of mass production/consumption and Keynesian regulation – catered for economic and social need across the social spectrum. Work and welfare were not the responsibility, in any significant sense, of the Third Sector or civil society in general.

Of course there were wide variations in experience between countries. Fordism was a hegemonic model, not a uniform practice. As such, in many countries where the combination of mass production, Keynesian regulation, and universal welfare did not prevail, small firms and the informal economy remained important sources of work and enterprise, as did households and Third Sector organisations for welfare provision. The normative goal under Fordism, however, was security through regular work and 'jobs for life', career mobility, consumption, and the all-providing state. One consequence of increasing state provision was substantial growth in public service sector employment. Another, less positive, one was that Fordism reduced the historical reliance on civil society for income and welfare security, and with this, the unpredictability, unevenness, and discontinuity of provision that came with dependence upon the voluntary sector. As a result, civil society came to be seen as the arena of self-help, associational activity and social life, not that of economic activity or preparation for it.

Fordism drew on an integrationist model of (national) society. Though it undoubtedly sharpened divisions along lines of class, gender, and ethnicity, it sat squarely within a modernist ideology of universal belonging: the right and desirability for everyone to be part of a society of universal work, consumption, and citizenship (Bauman 1998; Procacci 1999; Rose 1998). Fordism emphasised conformity to a shared set of norms rather than celebrating diversity. Poverty and other forms of social disadvantage were considered as temporary and to be eliminated through insertion into consumer society and the mores of societal/ group belonging. Needs and the needy, therefore, were still seen as part of a common social order; mass participation, after all, is what the economy required. They were not seen as a separate realm requiring special treatment, which, as we shall see, is an important difference from how social exclusion (an unfamiliar term during Fordism) is seen now.

Finally, Fordism symbolised a model of citizenship based on collective rights, distributive justice, and representative democracy. The social rights of citizens coalesced around struggles over income redistribution and the offerings of the welfare state. Their political demands centred around the universals of justice, fairness, and equality, fought through mass political parties, parliament, and other representative institutions. With the exception of notable mass organisations such as the trades unions, and periods of social mobilisation during late Fordism (e.g. the student and feminist movements), civil society was hollowed out as a zone of citizenship and political engagement. It became the zone of the social or the private; the sphere of social reproduction, opinion, morality, and ethics.

Cracks

By the mid 1970s, Fordism had become increasingly vulnerable as a societal model under the pressure of systematic challenges such as:

- rising global energy prices;
- rising imports from low-wage countries and flexibly organised new economies;
- wage drift and sustained opposition from organised labour;
- decreasing returns on sunk capital;
- growth of new technologies and organisational principles no longer dependent upon economies of scale;

- falling demand for mass-produced goods and the rise of customised consumption;
- waning support for mass/representative democracy;
- strains on the national regulatory state due to bureaucratic inefficiency, escalating welfare expenditure, the difficulty of managing trade and investment in an open international economy, and the rise of the market philosophy.

A first reaction by industry in the Fordist heartland was to restore profitability by relocating work to cheap labour zones, forcing mass redundancies, increasing labour productivity, and putting-out or subcontracting peripheral tasks. In the meantime, new industries such as micro-electronics and other high value-added or design-intensive industries appeared, able to compete with smaller workforces, flexible technologies, and flexible work practices. The effect – highlighted by the alarming rapidity of capacity reduction in the industrial regions of the developed economies in the early 1980s – was the transformation of work and the work ethic.

This is the first of two significant developments to rekindle interest in the social economy. Fordist deindustrialisation marked the end of full employment. It punctured the expectation of stable employment for all from the formal economy (Gorz 1982; Rifkin 1995). The 1980s 'naturalised' new labour market conditions. One of these was long-term unemployment due to productivity increases and the technological substitution of labour. Another was the rise of under-employment, manifest in the substantial growth of part-time, contingent and informal employment, as firms sought to reduce labour costs and rewrite the social contract with labour. A third aspect was the rise of job insecurity, exacerbated by job losses in the public sector linked to a new culture of privatisation and deregulation. Furthermore, there was a distinctive geography to these new labour market conditions, marked by devastation in the industrial heartlands.

In this situation, the Third Sector began to acquire a new meaning, as a supplementary source of employment and entrepreneurship. While during Fordism the unemployed had been considered as part of the reserve army of labour, they now faced the prospect of permanent or frequent exclusion from paid work. Those lacking the requisite skills, attitudes, and experience became the 'socially excluded', with no guarantee of reinsertion into the labour market (Byrne 1999). Economic growth would no longer guarantee their return to work. They were new social subjects, possibly with a role in the informal or black economy or Third Sector organisations covering services abandoned by the state or the private sector (Catterall *et al.* 1996; Borzaga and Maiello 1998; CEC 1998a). The Third Sector was now seen as a source of training, work experience, contact networks, sociability, and psycho-social support for future workers and entrepreneurs. The Fordist right-to-work ethic was giving way to a new means-to-work ethic, delivered also by the Third Sector.

The second development of significance for the social economy concerns the implications of the crisis of Fordism for universal state welfare. The slowdown of growth increased the demands on the welfare state (e.g. due to rising unemployment) but it also put a strain on the resources available to meet this demand. The changed economic circumstances challenged state commitment to income redistribution, direct management of the national economy, and the provision of universal education, health-care and social insurance. The 'yawning gap between expenditure and revenues' forced 'a rapid growth in the public sector borrowing requirement' (Pierson 1991: 146), a 'fiscal crisis of the state' (O'Connor 1973), which increasingly came to be viewed as unsustainable by governments. For example, in Britain, real social security spending (excluding pensions) grew by between 10–19 per cent in the early 1990s, while family credit claims doubled, housing benefit claims grew by 20 per cent and income support claims grew by 6 per cent a year (Davis 1999).

There were also other reasons for reconsidering the principle of a universal welfare state. First, capital's need for a national reserve army of labour had disappeared. As a result, governments could become much more selective about which sections of the labour market actively to reproduce and which sections of the economically inactive minimally to cater for so as to secure their consumption potential and contain their sense of social alienation. It was no surprise that business started to object against the use of tax revenue for universal welfare and income redistribution. Second, popular support for taxation also declined in the 1980s (Confalonieri and Newton 1995), due in part to what Galbraith (1992) described as the politics of a contented majority prepared to accept increases in social inequality. This new politics drew on a middle class self-concern that high taxation would yield incommensurate welfare benefits (especially so with the growth of private welfare schemes and personal savings). The welfare state was re-packaged as a choiceless option in a choice-based consumer society, possibly best suited in a cheap version for the 'shameful' poor (Bauman 1998). Third, political parties began to reject the idea of the all-providing state. Long-suffering neo-liberals who later became the New Right, grasped the moment to blame the welfare state for fostering a culture of dependency and entitlement (for example, in the UK, Thatcherites railed against 'the nanny state'). They called for market provision and discipline and individual motivation. But into the 1990s, social democrats too, looking for a 'third way' between state and market, and also concerned with the mounting welfare bill, accepted that the state should provide mainly for those most in need and that welfare entitlements should be coupled to responsibilities (e.g. workfare in Clinton's USA, welfare-to-work in Blair's Britain – see Blair 1997a; Giddens 1998).

The return of the social

The crisis of Fordism renewed interest in the potential of the social economy as a source of work and welfare. The stakes were high, as Jeremy Rifkin notes:

> The steady disengagement of government and commerce from communities around the world is leaving an ever widening institutional vacuum. That

vacuum is being filled in some cases by a rejuvenated third sector and, in other instances, by an emboldened fourth sector made up of the informal economy, the black market, and criminal culture. . . . for the third sector to prevail it will have to politicize itself by bringing various institutions, activities, and interests in a shared sense of common mission.

(2000: 245)

During the nineteenth century, the social economy was not seen as a weapon against poverty, which was considered to be natural and inevitable (Bauman 1998), but as a remedy for pauperism, understood as a state of moral turpitude. The social economy was driven by a set of moralising norms and philanthropic institutions for 'the undeserving' (Rose 1998). Some of the effort, as Giovanna Procacci (1978) has noted for late eighteenth and early nineteenth century France, involved encouraging informal activity for self-help. The social economy encapsulated a unity of labour and (moral) well-being for the poor. In an odd way, we have returned to this kind of approach in contemporary public policy discourse, around the idea that the Third Sector can deliver services for the socially excluded, by engaging the socially excluded, thereby meeting welfare need at the same time as stimulating work and social reengagement (Borzaga and Maiello 1998; Lipietz 1992, 1995; CEC 1998a). The premise is that the crisis of the welfare state potentially generates a huge market for the not-for-profit sector to deliver goods and services to help satisfy the largely under-met needs of excluded groups or communities. For example, the withdrawal of banks, businesses, shops, and the public sector from deprived neighbourhoods and communities owing to diminishing returns or the specificity of the welfare need within them, leaves an array of unmet needs. These range from access to child-care for young mothers and training opportunities for the unemployed, to care facilities for the elderly and a decent physical environment for the community as a whole. Equally under-met seem to be the composite needs of the unemployed, the stigmatised (e.g. immigrants, asylum seekers, the homeless, drug addicts), and the disadvantaged (e.g. ethnic minorities, single mothers, under-educated youth, disabled people). The function of the social economy, as a prominent UK activist puts it, is 'to turn needs into markets' (Grimes 1997).

For some commentators, the Third Sector is ideally suited to respond to these 'market' opportunities. Its commitment to welfare/social need rather than profit makes it an obvious protagonist of the new social economy (Pearce 1993; Grimes 1997; Ekins 1986, 1992). As Fasenfest *et al.* (1997: 15) put it: 'A social economy paradigm would wish to make a distinction between values which are monetized and those that are not'. Then, as they are generally light on resources, Third Sector organisations are seen as better able to cope with the economics of specialised provision (Anheier and Seibel 1990). Further, their commitment to combating social exclusion is said to give them a unique understanding of what it takes to help individuals to become active economic agents and citizens. Leadbeater (1997), for example, extols the rise of a new breed of energetic 'social entrepreneurs' based in the Third Sector.

The above neo-pauperism connects with a second, but much broader, aspect of contemporary interest in the social economy. This concerns its potential role in building social capital, that is, an ability and capacity in civil society to enhance economic efficiency and extend the democratic franchise through networks of inter-personal and collective engagement (Putnam 1993). Social enterprises in particular, and the Third Sector in general, as sites of both social reintegration and provision for social need, are increasingly seen as sources of social capital of a particular sort. There are different claims made, depending on moral and political stance. 'Civic conservatives', for whom 'the free market and limited government create the space in which all the institutions that stand between the individual and the state can grow and thrive' (Willetts 1999: 31), stress the virtue of self-responsibility. The social economy can inculcate an ideology of self-motivation and self-provision, helping to return individuals as free market agents. Many gains are expected, as Heidi Rimke elaborates:

> Self-help literature describes the self as the unified centre of personal agency which can act upon itself, others and the world. This conception presents the individual as the sole ontological pivot of experience. Further, the self is conceived as possessing an inner reservoir of power that can be accessed. This suggests an intense accountability, responsibility, and sense of obligation that can be enlisted for choices and decisions. . . . a mode of self-regulation which seeks to govern subjects in terms of their presumably 'personal' truths. . . .
>
> (2000: 64)

In contrast, US-based Communitarian thought (Etzioni 1973, 1995; Gittell and Vidal 1998; Walzer 1995), which has much to say about social exclusion, places the emphasis on a socially-generated morality and capacity to act, on the merits of welfare society, rather than welfare individualism. But the social is carefully defined: no longer the traditional social democratic emphasis on the social state and corporate social responsibility, but mutuality within homogeneous communities as an antidote for the damaging individualism and apathy to be found among the socially excluded. Here, the social economy is seen as part of a community-building project, helping to revitalise solidarity and reciprocity in localities of common ailment (e.g. inner city areas or outer estates of high unemployment and social deprivation), through demonstration projects that meet social need and inculcate values of mutuality.

Thus, a third expectation from the social economy is that it links with a new politics of grass-root empowerment or 'social justice from the bottom up' (Donnison 1994), after the Fordist legacy of mass, representative democracy. As Bucek and Smith note:

> Participation is at the heart of reforms to augment representative with direct democracy and to diversify methods of policy formation, service delivery, and other means of community and client involvement in the management of public services. For too long, participation in local affairs has been tokenistic,

involving little more than consultation with public opinion in ways which produce results that can easily be ignored by those in formal positions of local authority.

(2000: 14–15)

Two distinct readings of the social economy as a new model of participatory democracy can be identified. One centres on the redefinition of the public sphere, as the arena of active citizens (de Leonardis 1998). The users and beneficiaries of Third Sector initiatives are not simply future workers, welfare providers, and responsible individuals or communities (Hoggett 1997), but also active political subjects. They are potentially a significant voice in their often disempowered local communities (Donnison 1994), a voice for the economy of care and social entrepreneurship. The organisations of the social economy 'can empower people in a number of ways through their own participatory practices, through advocacy, interest articulation, and protest, and through alliances with similarly placed groups in other localities and cultures' (Bucek and Smith 2000: 12). The second reading emphasises the institutions of the social economy, within a model of associative democracy based on the distribution of power to interest organisations, specialised authorities and civic associations (Hirst 1994). In the stakeholder society the associative and institutional powers of the Third Sector can absorb welfare responsibilities as a consequence of state design or neglect (de Leonardis 1998), as well as develop a more open and collaborative code of practice with clients (Madanipour *et al.* 1998; Williams and Windebank 1998).

A fourth and very different expectation from the social economy supports a counter-culture of survival or transformation on the margins of capitalism. There is a long utopian tradition in favour of the organisation of society around needs, self-autonomy, and social and ecological balance. This utopian view reacts against the capitalist emphasis on individual greed, profit, and market value rather than social need. As Fordism slid into crisis, this counter-culture gained momentum through the student movement which campaigned for alternative communities, anti-establishment values and non-consumerist lifestyles; the women's movement, which rejected patriarchy in favour of new principles of solidarity and care; and parts of the labour movement, which pressed for workers' control and production for social utility. Some intellectuals even argued that 'the end of work' after Fordism offered a major opportunity to shift social organisation in this direction (Gorz 1999). However, there was never a sizeable shift in consciousness towards this alternative ethos, given the hold of work, income, and consumption in people's lives. However, the experience of unemployment and welfare withdrawal has spawned a variety of survival mechanisms which draw on non-market transactions and/or pooled resources of one sort or another (Fuller and Jonas 2002; North 1998; Lee 1996; Leyshon and Thrift 1997). These are also claimed as part of the social economy, run as they are by self-help groups and various Third Sector organisations. Ventures include alternative currency systems based on 'metered' time (e.g. time dollars) or vouchers; low-interest credit unions pooled from local contributions; local trading arrangements based on barter (e.g. two hours of child-care for one hour of tuition); and resources shared on a co-operative or communal basis (e.g. housing, food, recreation facilities). While only too often the ventures fall short of meeting the needs of people on the breadline, they are shot through with a culture of alterity.

The social economy, in summary, has acquired a number of raised expectations ranging from its role as a source of work, entrepreneurship and welfare, to its role in restoring community, associative democracy, and a counter-acquisitive culture. It is presented as the other face of an emerging fast capitalism marked by global consumerism, knowledge workers and knowledge entrepreneurs, giant corporations, flexible careers, and the culture of self-care (Sennett 1998; Rifkin 2000; Flores and Gray 2000).

International variations on a theme

There are considerable international differences in the ways in which the social economy and the relationship of the social economy to market, state, and civil society are envisioned. The ways in which the social economy is conceptualised and understood, and the ways in which it is seen to relate to social exclusion, have taken a variety of forms, partly reflecting varying national cultural and political traditions and policy choices (Jouen 2000: 15–26). Typically these are described in different terminologies and vocabularies. In the USA, '. . . a country characterised by a welfare system of a residual type . . . the distribution and production of goods and services was undertaken principally by . . . non-profit organisations' (Borzaga and Maiello 1998: 25). Reflecting the absence of a strong welfare state, there has been a well-established tradition of seeking to build a sense of community and encourage local 'bottom up' community development gradually distanced from the politically-inspired community activism in which it was originally rooted. The Third Sector became a new form of organising welfare via non-profit and voluntary organisations (for example, see Mollenkopf 1983). Elsewhere in north America – in Cape Breton in Canada, for example – there was a strong tradition of community economic development as the basis of a local social economy that sought to confront problems of catastrophic industrial decline and its associated ills in a peripheral region (see Lionais 2001).

In western Europe, in contrast, 'the apparently predominant view . . . is that recourse to private supply, especially when it replaces public supply, should be financed wholly or at least partly out of public funds' (Borzaga and Maiello 1998: 37). As a result, the state generally has taken a more prominent, though spatially and temporally variable, role in encouraging and supporting community and local economic development. Equally, it has been argued that the reductions in the scope of public expenditure and the welfare state in the last two decades have provided an important stimulus to the growth of a new socially-oriented entrepreneurship and, more generally, an expanded role for the social economy and Third Sector.[1] Within Europe, however, there was and is considerable variation. Echoing the identification of distinct forms of welfare capitalism (Hudson and Williams 1999: 9–15), the César Foundation has identified four models of the social economy in Europe: Anglo-Saxon, Mediterranean, Nordic, and Rhineland,[2] with important national variations within the latter three models. The Rhineland model encompasses Belgium, France, and Germany. In Germany 'the market social economy' comprises four subsectors: welfare associations, co-operatives, health mutuals, and a 'vast array of voluntary organisations and initiatives of all sorts', but it is argued that there is a general lack of awareness of the social economy and its potentialities. In contrast, France could perhaps be seen as the paradigmatic European case of a state-supported social economy '. . . due to the fact that organisations managing services on behalf of the state maintain that they should be remunerated because they are performing a public service' and the social enterprise has been accorded a specific legal status (*société à finalité sociale*: Borzaga and Maiello 1998: 36–7). The term social economy is accorded widespread recognition in France, with a liaison committee (CNLAMCA: National Liaison Committee for Co-Operatives, Mutuals and Associations) involving representatives from both government departments and social economy organisations. Belgium forms a hybrid, falling between the German and French cases, especially with regard to mutuals 'which are in fact an arm of government'. In many areas, especially education and hospital management, 'the state has delegated powers to the private sector, which it then finances'. In 1995, however, Belgium introduced the legal concept of a company set up for 'social purposes', indicative of a growing recognition of the potential role of the social economy.

The Nordic model as defined by the César Foundation comprises Finland, Norway, and Sweden. All three countries have very similar social systems: a solid tradition of popular movements, a large public sector, and a strong welfare state. Indeed, in Scandinavia, the 'free nature of services is still seen as an essential, almost ethical, element of the welfare system' (Borzaga and Maiello 1998: 35). Even so, there have been recent reductions in the level of public expenditure and in the scope of public sector provision of services but these have stimulated Third Sector activity and the growth of co-operatives, especially in rural areas. As a result, welfare provision and services are delivered via a more complex mix of state and social economy, with the reductions in the scope of state provision creating spaces which social economy organisations have occupied, often with state support. Denmark is a related though different case, with an innovative social economy and a long tradition of local co-operative development in regions such as Jutland that extends back well over a century (Dunford and Hudson 1996). Again, there is evidence of imaginative social economy projects emerging (for example in child care, education, and personal services), often enabled and helped via state support, despite a generally neo-liberal tone to national economic policy. As Borzaga and Maiello (1998: 35) note, 'the Scandinavian countries are altering their welfare systems only very slowly'. Furthermore, they are doing so in ways that demonstrate that development of the social economy can be reconciled and made compatible with a decent and generous welfare system as part of a pro-gressive politics of redistribution.

The Mediterranean model is defined by the César Foundation as comprising Italy, Portugal, and Spain. The Foundation emphasises that there is no doubt that Italy is the European country where the Third Sector is strongest. It is made up of co-operatives, third world NGOs and non-profit associations. The organisation of the sector is driven politically by the Third Sector Forum, which functions as a debating chamber and a political lobby, and has just been admitted to employer–employee negotiations.

Since 1991, the social enterprise has been accorded a specific legal status: *cooperativa sociale* (Borzaga and Maiello 1998: 36–7). In contrast, the social economy is relatively underdeveloped in Portugal and Spain It was only in 1999, for example, that Portugal introduced the legal concept of 'social co-operatives with limited liability'. In the case of Greece, the Report asks: 'can we really talk of a third sector?' This is a reflection of the much greater role of the extended family in social reproduction over much of mediterranean Europe. As the Report concludes, 'In sum, there is no real Mediterranean model. There is however an Italian model, along with very disparate situations in Spain, Greece and Portugal'.

The Anglo-Saxon model in Europe is unique to the UK, with a particular emphasis upon tackling social exclusion, defined as a locally-specific condition, via local social economy and 'Third Sector' approaches, encompassing a variety of co-operatives, credit unions, traditional mutuals, voluntary organisations, socially-oriented business and housing associations. This has become a central element in the political-economy of New Labour, and we explore this in more detail in Chapter 2, reflected both in the writings of Prime Minister Blair (see Blair 1997a) and his intellectual apologists (such as Giddens 1998, 2000). For the moment we simply note that the social economy is seen as 'very dynamic' and as an integral part of a Third Way between state and market, meeting socio-political aims via socially useful economic activity. It encompasses the production and distribution of goods and services in this way and as a consequence creates alternative forms of work and employment, as well as in other respects seeking to create such employment as its primary goal. The social economy is seen to comprise organisations that are largely locally-owned and controlled and, as such, to promote local democracy – the 'localisation' of the social economy is a critical issue and one discussed more fully below. New Labour's Third Way thus draws both upon aspects of the European and north American traditions, as well as more recent policy propositions emerging from the European Commission. For example, the close linkage between work and personal responsibility can be found in the Clinton Administration's version of the Third Way, through such legislation as the 1996 Personal Responsibility and Work Opportunities Reconciliation Act and a host of state and locally-based workfare schemes. They find resonance in New Labour thinking and policy (Peck and Theodore 1999).

Panacea or problem?

Despite the national variations, in all of the above interpretations, the social economy emerges as a creature of either necessity or desire. The pragmatic case stresses the unavoidable need to restore the social as a source of jobs and welfare.

This raises important questions – pursued in this book through evidence on the UK – concerning the ability of the social economy to deliver. Does the Third Sector, for example, have to provide sustainable support, hampered as it is by limited finances, voluntary effort and multiple demands? What, then, will stop a civic-based welfare system becoming one of 'ad hoc conjunctural rules instead of universal rules of justice' (Procacci 1999: 26), a highly uneven and unpredictable source of jobs and welfare? Indeed, what services are on offer – do they simply cosmetically plaster over the cracks of welfare deprivation or do they provide genuinely useful services? And, what kinds of jobs – short-term work for a modest number of people or capacity-building for more permanent and rewarding employment? Is there, finally, a sustainable market for services in between the mainstream economy and the state, to enable the social economy to exist as a sphere in its own right? The case for necessity, thus, remains largely unproven.

The normative case seems to be grounded, as already implied, in anxiety about the loss of a society of commitments (Sennett 1998). Jeremy Rifkin, for example, in reference to 'a rejuvenated third sector', claims:

> If the workings of global networks, cyberspace commerce, and cultural production represent one side of a new politics of power in the coming century, then the reestablishment of deep social exchange, the recreation of social trust and social capital, and the restoration of strong geographic communities represent the other side. The contrarian rallying cry, in an era increasingly given over to short-lived facile connections, virtual realities, and commodified experiences, is that geography counts! Culture matters!
>
> (2000: 256)

Similarly, Richard Sennett (1998: 139) argues 'the fictive "we" has come to life again, to defend against a vigorous new form of capitalism', because 'one of the unintended consequences of modern capitalism is that it has strengthened the value of place, aroused a longing for community'. Enter the values of the social economy, as Charles Leadbeater asserts:

> To create a modern sense of community we need to open up public spaces where people with diverse interests, skills and resources can meet, debate, listen and co-operate to find common purposes and develop shared values. The private sector is skilled at bringing together a diversity of people as consumers, generally for a commercial purpose. Despite the best efforts of many hard-pressed managers and workers, too often the welfare state seems to divide people rather than bring them together.
>
> (1997: 24)

There seems to be a new politics of hope here based on the powers of community, civic agreement, and a yearning for a home called place. In it, the social economy, as the sphere of welfare and work in the hands of the Third Sector and the community, is expected to be at centre stage.

How are we to judge this subtle reinvention of the social and the civic as (place-based) community? In the academic literature, there is mounting criticism of a version of the new politics of hope which seeks community for the socially excluded. This version, which is particularly germane to our concerns, is seen to conceal an exclusionary politics that associates the poor and poverty with particular types of people, places and modes of intervention. There are three strands to the critique. First, as Giovanna Procacci notes, the language of social exclusion presupposes societal separation:

> This means that poverty is analysed as a marginal condition, characteristic of drop-outs, and becomes the state of living if one falls outside society, rather than a predicament which can occur within society – the condition of marginalized people, rather than a process of creating and maintaining inequality, a process rooted in social structure. [. . .] It pretends to eject out of society the problems producing poverty. Vulnerability, precariousness of work, diminishing resources, weakening of social protections – all processes that intensify the polarization of society well before the threshold into extreme poverty is crossed.
>
> (1999: 24)

A second criticism is that any redrawing of the boundary between insiders and outsiders, the deserving and the undeserving, allows the welfare problem to be marked as a special case for selective treatment of only some people, when contrasted with the principle of provision for all enshrined in the universal welfare state. There are many demarcations at work, including the acceptance of the poor in badly paid or insecure jobs, and the banishment of the very poor from the 'universe of moral obligation' (Bauman 1998: 72), or their pathologisation:

> The kind of policies that social exclusion has implemented are mainly characterized by turning social problems into *urban problems*. . . . Therefore, the unique meaning of citizenship at work in such policies is *local integration*. From this vantage point citizenship, or lack of it, becomes a question of sociability, at most a question of 'active animation', a culture, an identity, a set of behaviours whose frame is the urban location where the exclusion takes place [. . .] Localism does not represent the resentment of being no longer treated as a citizen; it only reinforces the sense of exclusion by pretending that problems of the poor are no longer a collective issue, a public concern.
>
> (Procacci 1999: 24–5, emphasis in original)

Third, therefore, the critical literature highlights the old sociological distinction between communal versus societal belonging/obligation. In the idea of community, the poor, in their own homogeneous localities, are treated as not like the rest of us and in need of 'conversion' to become citizens. The idea of society, instead, treats them as one of us, as citizens entitled to the social and political rights enjoyed by the rest of us. It warns, as Procacci alludes, of the real danger of ghettoisation and resentment – not the communitarian ideal of fellowship – that goes with the identification of poverty with a particular community. It emphasises fellowship and citizenship within a differentiated, but single, social formation (Sennett 1998). And, it warns of the only too easy step that it takes for the state to disengage from universal welfare obligations in a discourse that focuses on particular groups. As Paul Hoggett notes for the British case, 'during the period from the mid 1980s onwards, we can see how "community" became a metaphor for the absence or withdrawal of services by the state' (1997: 10).

Conclusion

The Third Sector has become a symbol of the return of civil society into economic and political life; a significant source of work, welfare, and participatory democracy in a new stage of capitalism. Much is expected from the social economy it can animate. The latter merits serious attention. What we make of it, however, is not uncontroversial. We are seeing two very contrasting interpretations. On the one hand, the positive account sees the social economy as a unitary source of work and welfare, and a zone of social engagement through its inculcation of skills, community values, and the responsible subject. Nothing other than good can come from it.

The cautionary account, on the other hand, links the rise of the social economy to an erosion of the 'social' or universal welfare state, commitment to social justice as desirable in itself and the principle of the inclusive society. Let us summarise the argument. First, the rise of the Third Sector provides an opportunity for the state to reduce its welfare commitments in the face of rising fiscal stress and a mounting anti-welfare ideology (Rose 1998: 66). Second, state interest in plural sources of provision is a step towards accepting uneven welfare provision, a radical shift from the assumption that, as Smith puts it:

> . . . all persons share natural characteristics, generating needs which must be satisfied to live a human life, the wherewithal for which might be claimed as a human right. This position has strong egalitarian implications, for if the natural characteristics, needs, and rights are universal in the sense of applying to everyone everywhere, there is no moral reason why some people in some places should be better supplied than others with sources of need satisfaction.
> (2000: 1155)

Third, in the new welfare governmentality, recipients are seen as pathologically different from the mainstream; the fallen/depraved in deprived areas/dangerous places, from whom new obligations must be extracted. Chillingly, Rose observes:

> It appears as if, outside the communities of inclusion, exists an array of micro-sectors, micro-cultures of non-citizens, failed citizens, anti-citizens, comprised of those who are unable or unwilling to enterprise their lives or manage their own risk, incapable of exercising responsible self-government,

either attached to no moral community or to a community of anti-morality. It is in relation to these marginal and pathological persons that one sees the emergence of a new politics of conduct, which re-unifies the abjected subjects ethically and spatially. Ethically, in that they are accorded a new active relation to their status in terms of their strategies and capacities for the management of themselves: they have either refused the bonds of civility and self responsibility, or they aspire to them but have not been given the skills, capacities and means. And spatially in that the unified space of the social is re-configured, and the abjected are re-located, in both the imagination and strategy, in 'marginalised' spaces: in the decaying council estate, in the chaotic lone parent family, in the shop doorways of inner city streets.

(1998: 79)

This book explores where the balance lies by drawing on a body of original research on the experience of the social economy in different parts of the UK.

2 Social economy, social exclusion, localisation

Introduction

In the previous chapter we showed how the concept of the social economy rose to prominence in the context of the crisis of Fordism as a model of socio-economic development and regulation. This led to more widespread and intensified forms of socio-spatial differentiation, with significant concentrations of poverty and multiple deprivation that increasingly became swept up under the rubric of 'social exclusion'. In turn, given the perceived limitations of mainstream policy responses to the problems of the socially excluded, this led to an accelerating search for new modes of state policy formation and implementation to tackle increasingly generalised but localised social exclusions. In this context, there was growing interest in the social economy and/or Third Way as alternative policy approaches (Birkholzer 1996). Not least, as they were seen as making relatively small demands on public expenditure: 'The big money goes to mainstream economic re-generation: only in smaller and less well-resourced local partnerships is a social economy approach significant' (Geddes 2000: 797). It was in this context that the social economy increasingly became defined as the solution to problems of social exclusion. Even more significantly, this equation has depended upon a further manoeuvre – the localising of both social exclusion and the social economy, with both understood as constituted at the local level. The net result is to create an elision between 'social exclusion', 'social economy', and the 'local'; indeed, to equate 'social exclusion' as the problem and 'social economy' as the policy solution precisely via defining them both as necessarily constituted at the local level.

In this chapter, first, we review the emergence and recent history of the concept of social exclusion, and the way in which social exclusion has been defined as a problem at the local scale and the localisation of the social economy has become defined as the solution to this problem within the discourses of Third Way politics. Then we go on to illustrate how this particular treatment of the social economy has been taken up in EU policy discourse on social exclusion. Finally, we examine the coupling of social exclusion and social economy via a more detailed look at the case of New Labour in the UK, posed increasingly (certainly in terms of its self-perception and publicity) as the paradigmatic Third Way project defining the politics of the new millennium. The ring to the chapter is that the 'exceptionalism' of the emerging EU/UK approach when set in the context of the international variations we outlined in Chapter 1, could become a new orthodoxy.

Social exclusion: a community problem?

The concept of social exclusion has a short but well-documented history. The invention of the term is commonly attributed to René Lenoir, the French Minister for Social Action. In 1974 he referred in a speech to *les exclus* – 10 per cent of the French population that he claimed were existing beyond civil society because they were not covered by social insurance. They included: 'the mentally and the physically handicapped, suicidal people, aged invalids, abused children, drug addicts, delinquents, single parents, multi-problem households, marginal, asocial persons, and other social misfits' (Silver 1994: 532).

Interestingly, given the subsequent history of the term, this list encompasses a wide range of individual conditions and problems and social ills and pathologies but does not explicitly refer to the unemployed or any other group whose exclusion might be attributed primarily to *economic* deprivation. To some extent, this can be related to the emergence of the concept towards the end of the long period of 'full employment' in Europe. However, the broadening of social exclusion to include economic deprivation happened very quickly in response to rapid changes in the structure of European economy and society. The term was appropriated by the French Left to describe both 'the ones that economic growth forgot' during periods of expansion, and subsequently the growing numbers of the unemployed and the poor that accompanied the recessions of the late 1970s and 1980s (Silver 1994: 534–5).

As Allen suggests, the end product of this process of on-going redefinition is that:

> What appears to be new in this situation is the social multi-dimensionality of poverty and *precarité*, so that age, gender, race, migration, household structure, educational qualification, etc. form a set of lines along which peripheralisation and potential exclusion from the labour force can run.
>
> (1998: 28)

Social exclusion – since it encompasses a range and depth of mutually-reinforcing problems – does not simply describe the static condition of 'poverty' or 'deprivation' but emphasises the *processes* by which aspects of social marginalisation are intensified over time. As such, social exclusion is a powerful concept encapsulating the cumulative effects of multiple disadvantage and social exclusion can be manifest in numerous, often inter-related, ways: cultural, economic, political, and spatial. For example, it is often difficult for marginal communities to gain access to processes of political decision-making from which they may be culturally, educationally, and linguistically, as well as physically, remote. In addition to direct discriminatory practices such as racism, sexism, 'ableism', and ageism, there is a plethora of more subtle processes of socio-cultural marginalisation. Even so, the single most commonly cited source of poverty and social exclusion remains unemployment (see Chapter 1). The resultant denial of access to economic resources has been the most commonly cited proximate cause of social exclusion in the core territories of industrial capitalism in which unemployment has been a persistent problem since the 1970s. Without suggesting that other forms of social exclusion are reducible to a lack of waged work, there is no doubt that they are often linked to it. This is a view that is now prevalent in policy circles over north America and Europe and defines social exclusion predominantly in terms of economic exclusion (Levitas 1996).

Social exclusion is also understood as scaled in particular ways. Geddes emphasises the '"spatiality" of social exclusion' and refers to a

> New geography of deprivation and problems of disorder (crime and fear of crime) associated with economic, physical and social degradation in many urban neighbourhoods . . . certain spatial dimensions of social exclusion are particularly prominent in the 1990s. These include those concentrations of the poor in large public (Fordist) housing estates, but also in other urban locations frequently cheek by jowl with affluence, including neighbourhoods with large migrant and/or ethnic populations or 'racial ghettos' and remoter rural regions. In such areas, alienated younger people, especially young males, are frequently portrayed as out of control, terrorizing 'ordinary citizens'.
>
> (2000: 783)

Although the socially excluded are understood to be excluded from the mainstream national, and by extension global, labour market, their point of (re)entry is almost without exception understood to be 'local'. For example, Borzaga (n.d.: 1) refers to the growth of the Third Sector 'as a consequence of the demand for the integration of excluded people at the local level', without offering any explanation of why this demand is seen to be one that is necessarily situated at the local level. This taken-for-granted 'localness' is, in fact, central to the construction of the standard representation of social exclusion that ascribes to it a specific spatial scale: that of the local community. Empirically, this is quite understandable in terms of describing manifestations of poverty and deprivation. The acute and compounded forms of social and material deprivation that the term social exclusion is used to describe tend to be concentrated in particular marginalised geographical areas. There is a familiar imagery associated with accounts of social exclusion in northern Europe and north America in particular, that includes rundown housing estates (both inner city and outer suburban social housing), scarred and shuttered town centres, and littered and graffittied streets.[1]

With social exclusion scaled in these ways, the 'local' has also become equated with 'community' (as we indicated in Chapter 1). As a consequence, and via a further slippage, the word 'community' has almost become a synonym for social exclusion. Hoggett makes the point emphatically: 'For policy makers and street-level bureaucrats within the state the idea of community has nearly always been used as a form of shorthand for the socially excluded' (1997: 11).

As a consequence, the debate on the causes and locations of social exclusion, as well as proposed solutions, has become cast in terms of geographically-defined communities and/or 'neighbourhoods' (Social Exclusion Unit 1998; CEC 1998a,b; Gittell and Vidal 1998; Levitas 1998; Madanipour *et al.* 1998; Byrne 1999). Perhaps the clearest expression of this is the way in which the solutions to social exclusion have been presented both by grassroots development agencies and Non-Governmental Organisations (NGOs) and, increasingly, by the institutions of national and international governance. As Byrne notes:

> 'Community' matters not just because it is the key collective identity constituted through space, but also because 'community' development has been just about the only strategy of empowerment attempted, however half-heartedly and sometime [*sic*] with a view to disempowerment rather than empowerment in the whole repertoire of anti-exclusion policy.
>
> (1999: 111)

The growing policy interest in localised solutions to social exclusion via local social economy initiatives has stimulated the creation of a number of databases documenting experiences, typically linked to ideas of 'best practice' and its (alleged) transferability between places. For example, both the United Nations Educational, Scientific and Cultural Organisation (UNESCO) and the EU have produced such databases. Many of the anti-exclusion projects recorded in the UNESCO database are concentrated in particular localities. In the case of the EU's Local Initiatives to Combat Social Exclusion in Europe (LOCIN) database, the 'localness' of the projects was a basic criterion of selection for inclusion. Micro-enterprises as promoted by the United States Agency for International Development Microenterprise Innovation Project (USAID MIP) are by definition highly localised. The result is that a 'new localism' (Goetz and Clarke 1993) has developed alongside the policy discourse of social exclusion in which 'community rules' (Levitas 1998). Indeed, it might be more accurate to claim that the 'new localism' has developed as an integral part of the discourse of social exclusion.

Linking social exclusion and the social economy through the local

As noted in Chapter 1, the social economy embraces a wide range of activities and a variety of organisational forms that may be non-hierarchical, using both waged workers and unwaged volunteers, and more democratic than those of the formal economy and state. It is becoming seen as a holistic solution for social exclusion in a number of ways. First, by encouraging collective self-help, confidence and capacity building, and nurturing the collective values of the economy via socially useful production. Second, by humanising the economy via an emphasis upon autonomy, associational values, and organising the economy at a 'human' scale. Third, by enhancing democracy and participation via a decentralisation of policy to local communities and places.[2] Fourth, by bringing about a greater degree of systemic coherence to the local economy via the local production and consumption of goods and services (*a fortiori* if this is linked to the creation of a local currency). Fifth, by acknowledging the relationships between economy, environment, politics, and society.

The linkage between the social economy and social exclusion – through evocations of community and local connectivity – is increasingly justified through the specificity of problems at the local level. The localised concept of the social economy emphasises the ability to address specific local needs and tackle localised social exclusion. Laville (1996, cited in Borzaga n.d.: 9–10) comments that a feature of social enterprises is 'their desire to promote a sense of social responsibility and further democracy at local level through economic activity'. The 'local' in this context, though rarely explicitly defined, usually refers to a small definable territory and a homogenous resident population – usually either a single housing estate, an established inner-city or suburban area or a rural village. Local social economy organisations are understood to be 'community-owned' organisations. They are seen to share a commitment to harness local economic activity and latent entrepreneurial capacity to create jobs and socially useful services by responding to the needs of the local, spatially delimited community (see, *inter alia*, Pearce 1993; Catterall *et al.* 1996; Gittell and Vidal 1998; CEC 1998a,b; Ekins and Newby 1998; Greffe 1998; Haughton 1999; Social Exclusion Unit 1998; DETR 1998). Such organisations allow a 'joint construction of supply and demand' (Laville 1996, cited in Borzaga n.d.: 14). So, for example, instead of local housing maintenance work being carried out by staff employed by a local authority or, as has been increasingly the case in the UK, by a private company on contract to the local authority, community-owned non-profit enterprises are established within housing estates to provide a more immediate and flexible service run by and for local people and to create jobs in the local economy (Saunders 1997).

The social economy is, therefore, conceptualised as an aggregation of localised Third Sector organisations, ready and able to combat localised social exclusion. For 'the social economy approach makes clear the extent to which alterations in the division of labour between monetized economic activity and non-monetized activity depends on the local context and culture' (Fasenfest *et al.* 1997: 16). As a consequence, the 'national' and, reflecting well-established or more recent forms of regional devolution in a range of advanced capitalist states, 'regional' social economies may be simply heterogeneous agglomerations of localised practices.

Making the local link: the EU dimension

This turn to the local is particularly evident in EU thinking on the social economy. Following the establishment of the Social Economy Unit within DG XXIII in 1989 (Molloy *et al.* 1999), the European Commission has paid increasing attention to the problems of social exclusion and to the social economy as a way of tackling them. The Commission sees this as a way forward for tackling widespread poverty and social exclusion that is compatible with the demands of a formal sector economy confronted with the challenges of new and more intense forms of global competition. For example, the White Paper on *Competition, Growth and Employment* expresses this point very clearly:

> Given the scale of the needs that have to be met, both in the European Union and elsewhere in the world, recovery must be achieved by developing work and employment and not by endorsing basically Malthusian [that is, welfare – the authors] solutions. [We must] remain faithful to the ideals which have come to characterise and represent Europe, of finding a new synthesis of the aims pursued by society (work as a factor of social integration, equality of opportunity) and the requirements of the economy (competitiveness and job creation).[3]
>
> (CEC 1994)

The concept of the 'third system' has recently been adopted as a formal policy strategy by the European Commission and European Parliament. It is deliberately vaguely specified, so that it can explicitly subsume a variety of different terms with broadly the same meaning:

> Third system, third sector, social economy, community development, local development and employment initiatives, local and territorial pacts for employment, endogenous local development, sustainable economy . . . the abundance of terms used to describe a group of innovative phenomena shows the current froth around a set of largely unknown realities.
>
> (CEC 1998b: 4)

While these realities may be presented as 'unknown', this has not stopped the Commission from proffering the following definition of organisations in the 'third system':

> These organisations aim to find *solutions* rather then [*sic*] to place themselves in a new market sector;
> They often refer to factors such as *social solidarity*, democratic organisations or the primacy of the individual over capital;
> These organisations are often the result of *public/private* partnerships and have a close relationship with their *local communities*;
> The market is not their sole source of income with organisations securing public subsidies, donations or loans – they often have very *mixed income*;
> Specific attention is often given to *disadvantaged* people by these organisations;
> These organisations are often small scale structures often with larger numbers of non-active associates or unpaid *volunteers*.
> Finally, the most important factor which justifies the growing interest in this type of initiative naturally concerns their close relationship to the development of new types of jobs, mainly linked to satisfying new personal

and collective needs which neither the public nor the market can currently meet.

(1998b: 6, emphases in original)

This specification of the attributes of 'third system' activities emphasises that they involve communitarian solutions that fall between state and market, and that they offer a potential palliative to the problems of disadvantaged people and places.[4] They are proposed as a model for policy convergence across the European Union. As Borzaga and Maiello note, 'it is possible to discern a sort of local convergence between initiatives to combat long-term employment and social enterprise', where the Commission could seek to 'promote the spread of quality [best] practice in the social enterprise' (1998: 40). With 'local' as 'national' taken out of the frame, it comes back, however, in the form of an acknowledgement of dynamics at the level of neighbourhoods and localities. The Commission is clearly suggesting that there is a local specificity both to the problems of disadvantage (of social exclusion) and the social economy initiatives through which these can be tackled. Thus, via processes of slippage, elision and assertion, social exclusion and the social economy have become defined as locally constituted, as sharing the same local places. A new hegemony of the social as local seems to be in the making. Nowhere has this been pushed with so much vigour than in Blair's Britain.

A paradigmatic case: New Labour and the Third Way

In this section we focus upon the complex relationships between New Labour, social exclusion, and the social economy. We do so not only to set the UK empirical evidence in this book in its policy context, but also because the Third Way politics of New Labour are presented by their protagonists as a new paradigmatic model of development for the new millennium (one with a strong resonance with EU policy shifts). The local social economy is presented as part of the solution to problems of social exclusion, the means through which the norms of the market economy can be made compatible with a socially-inclusive society in the UK. These are strong claims, given added significance by their elevation as part of a new paradigm of modern socio-economic development that is seen to be of general relevance and applicability.

The transformation from Old to New Labour, leading to the election of the 'New' Labour government on 1 May 1997, involved a significant ideological shift, embedded in a new political 'philosophy', the Third Way, intended to represent a radical departure from the atrophied politics of Right and Left (Giddens 1998). A form of corporatist and statist socialism associated with large-scale industrial production and universal welfare provision by the state was abandoned as New Labour joyously embraced the new 'realities' of globalisation, post-Fordism, flexible labour relations and a more fragmentary, service-based and volatile labour market. At the same time, the Third Way sought to distance itself from the burgeoning distributional inequalities of Thatcherite neo-liberalism. As such, the concept of social exclusion for the first time became central to national policy (Levitas 1998). The concepts of globalisation and social exclusion took central and related roles in the definition of 'modern', 'moral', and 'liberal' approaches to policy in general and anti-poverty and regeneration strategies in particular. These changes are explored through their central and recurrent themes – modernity, morality, and localism.

Much of the modernism of New Labour stems from a perceived need to reinvent the party as one of fiscal prudence, entrepreneurial zeal and strong business orientation, committed to markets as allocative institutions. None the less, New Labour's embracing of the market is tempered by the central claim of the Third Way that necessary participation in and adaptation to the global economy can be reconciled with a commitment to social justice and welfare. As Blair puts it: 'A key challenge of progressive politics is to use the state as an *enabling* force, protecting effective communities and voluntary organisations and encouraging their growth to tackle new needs, in partnership as appropriate' (1997a: 4, emphasis added).

The Third Way is central to an ongoing renegotiation of the state's role with regard to a transformed economy and a less fixed and coherent conception of civil society. If the former can be explained and 'managed' by constituting it as external and global, the latter remains the responsibility of the state.

The 'aspirations to succeed' with which Blair wishes to equip the citizens of the UK derive from what he calls his 'ethic of responsibility'. In addition to various Christian Socialist and Communitarian thinkers, Blair's views are influenced by Giddens (1998: 65), who proposes the motto 'no rights without responsibilities' as the basic ethical principle of the new politics. Reflecting this, Blair defines responsibility as a key value of the Third Way.

> For too long, the demand for rights from the state was separated from the duties of citizenship and the imperative for mutual responsibility on the part of individuals and institutions. Unemployment benefits were often paid without strong reciprocal obligations; children went unsupported by absent parents. . . . The rights we enjoy reflect the duties we owe; rights and opportunity without responsibility are engines of selfishness and greed.
>
> (1997a: 4)

Both Blair and Giddens see strong civic cultures, based on and developing from active and willing participation in collective activities, as central to their vision of the Third Way. However, both also see the role of the state as one of *enforcing* the acceptance of civil responsibilities; presumably in the hope that once set in motion via a cathartic one-off burst of state coercion, an inclusive civil society will come into being and subsequently reproduce itself via its own efforts. This is most clearly expressed in the Government's description of the objective of welfare reform: 'work for those who can and security for those who cannot' (DSS 1998: iii). What this means in practice is sanctions and inducements to compel welfare claimants to accept paid work or training places either in the 'mainstream' private sector economy or through a range of temporary, subsidised 'workfare' options through welfare-to-work (Peck 1998a,b). In this regard, the Third Way is a route back to employment in the formal economy for those who can – and must – take advantage of the opportunities it offers. Redefining citizenship as having a job necessitates policies to get the unemployed back into work in the mainstream formal labour market, with scant regard for the quality of such jobs as they might come to occupy. Responsibility, then, becomes responsibility for finding and securing paid work with the result that the unemployed, single mothers and the disabled are less dependent on, and therefore less of a burden on, the state as it seeks to promote the national territory to attract global capital.

In the new moral economy it is not only necessary but 'better' to work, however. If 'the mainstream economy – with its opportunities and risks – [is] the main path out of exclusion for all people of working age',[5] then social exclusion becomes the rubric under which those unable to seize those opportunities or bear the risks can be summarily dumped. For the socially excluded, however, the social economy is offered as the alternative source of work. For those who fail to get jobs in the mainstream economy, the Third Way offers a route to a world of survival via sequential training schemes, temporary employment and the possibility of work in the social economy. This preoccupation with finding work for people in some form or other reflects, as we flagged in Chapter 1, the fear that long-term structural unemployment may erode the work ethic and the habit of work, reinforce expectations of welfare and open the door to social disruption and societal problems (Byrne 1999; Bauman 1998).

In addition to being responsible for participation in the economy, citizens of the 'new Britain' bear responsibility for creating and maintaining civil society, encouraged and, if need be, enforced by state action:

> Strong communities depend on shared values and a recognition of the rights and duties of citizenship – not just the duty to pay taxes and obey the law, but the obligation to bring up children as competent, responsible citizens, and to support those – such as teachers – who are employed by the state in the task. In the past we have tended to take such duties for granted. But where they are neglected, we should not hesitate to encourage *and even enforce them*, as we are seeking to do with initiatives such as our 'home–school contracts' between schools and parents.
>
> (Blair 1997a: 12, emphasis added)

The redistribution of responsibility appears in many different forms throughout the New Labour agenda. All the documents relating to the 'New Contract for Welfare' (a title which alludes to contractarian notions of reciprocity) emphasise that delivering welfare reform is as much the responsibility of claimants as it is of the state (DSS 1998). It is even more pronounced in relation to the government's flagship employment programme, Welfare-To-Work, the core of the *New Deal*. This provides a subsidised, six-month work placement for the long-term unemployed in a range of private, public, and voluntary sector organisations in the hope and expectation that the participants will either then become employed permanently in the organisations in which they are placed, or, at the very least, will have been made more 'employable'.[6] 'Full employability' is now the goal rather than 'full employment'. Despite the claims, the evidence that such workfare schemes produce positive employment outcomes is, however, very ambiguous (Peck 1998a,b; Peck and Theodore 1999). This is the case in terms both of quantity and quality of jobs.

In terms of job quality, Byrne (1999) argues that supply-side measures such as those of *New Deal* do little to address issues of quality and in fact may institutionalise low pay. Accepting the fundamental association of social exclusion with unemployment does not mean supporting a view that tackling social exclusion can be exclusively equated with insertion into the wage relation, especially given contemporary labour market conditions in the UK (Geddes 2000: 795). As to the amount of jobs, evidence has shown that Welfare-to-Work produces large numbers of 'missing' people who drop out of the scheme either into insecure short-term jobs and then back into unemployment, or who are forced into a combination of poverty and the black economy. Of the 140,000 people participating in the scheme up to June 1999, 35 per cent had 'disappeared' in this way (Inman 1999). Considerable numbers get jobs through the scheme but often for relatively short periods. This is deeply problematic, not least in terms of the stated intentions of *New Deal*. In its Fifth Report into *New Deal* and Welfare-To-Work, the House of Commons Select Committee on Education and Employment expressed its concerns:

> that the proportion of moves into unsustained employment remains as high as 40 per cent. As the minister has told us on more than one occasion, young people on the *New Deal* are ambitious and aspirational and the *New Deal* has to be aspirational for them. Those aspirations will not be met by a cycle of continual short-term employment in entry-level jobs, unemployment and participation in the *New Deal*.
>
> (paragraph 40, p. xv, 2001)

As such, the Welfare-To-Work scheme seems to have reinforced labour market inequality, leaving a substantial subsection of the long-term unemployed with little or no access to secure employment, and therefore recycled within the social economy and confined within a minimal welfare system. The social economy risks becoming a mechanism for reinserting some of the unemployed into the mainstream labour market and a mechanism of surveillance and control over those who fail to make this transition.

There is also an intractably uneven geography to all of this. Schemes such as Welfare-To-Work rely on the capacity of the private sector economy to absorb unemployment and so, it has been argued, tend to reproduce and even exacerbate the existing uneven geography of employment (Peck 1998a). When they produce large numbers of positive employment outcomes, these tend to be concentrated in areas with relatively buoyant economies. Where unemployment is highest, because local labour-market dynamics are weakest, workfare schemes have had at best a marginal effect (Peck 1998a; Peck and Theodore 1999). Paradoxically though, it is in these locations that social economy initiatives are seen to have a key role in providing work and services for their socially excluded and marginalised residents. The question this raises is whether this comes as a sticking plaster over the most open wounds of a divided society rather than as a corrective to its dominant political–economic processes.

New Labour, New Localism: the *National Strategy for Neighbourhood Renewal* and the *New Deal for Communities*

In the Third Way, the harnessing of the local community is central to the 'reinvention' of the nation, the creation of an inclusive society, and particularly to tackling social exclusion. The local community is both the site at which the phenomenon of social exclusion is manifest and is presumed to be the most appropriate site of policy intervention. Under New Labour, if social exclusion 'happens' at the level of the local community, the latter is therefore responsible for its alleviation. The main expressions of this have emerged from the strategy and policy documents produced by the Social Exclusion Unit, *Bringing Britain Together: A National Strategy for Neighbourhood Renewal* and the *New Deal for Communities.*

The Social Exclusion Unit (SEU) was established in December 1997 to create inter-departmental synergies within government and generate innovative policies to combat the 'very modern problem' of social exclusion as the concept became central to the mainstream policy debate in the UK (Blair 1997b: 2). The SEU 'reports direct to the Prime Minister and is located within the Cabinet Office, putting it at the heart of Government' (SEU 2001: 58). Its members were drawn from relevant government departments (health, social security, education and employment, and environment, transport and the regions), the private sector (National Westminster Bank), statutory agencies (the Probation Service, the Police), NGOs (Crime Concern, Church Urban Fund), a local authority, and a member of the Prime Minister's 'No.10 Policy Unit' (SEU 1998). Beyond the responsibilities of those working directly within the Unit, a network of government ministers was established to enable the SEU to access the policy-making process, and eighteen Policy Action Teams (PATs) were formed to co-ordinate research and policy formation.[7] The Unit was established for two years in the first instance and given a timetable of activities covering a set of agreed priorities; namely, truancy and school exclusions, rough sleeping and what were dubbed 'worst estates'. The activities of the SEU were reviewed after two years and its life extended until the end of 2002, at which point a further review will occur (SEU 2001: 58).

The first outcomes of the Unit's work emerged in September 1998 with the publication of *Bringing Britain Together: A National Strategy for Neighbourhood Renewal* and the *New Deal for Communities*, the first major policy initiative from the Unit. Although the *National Strategy* specifically prioritised tackling the 'worst estates', it was also a statement of the overall strategy direction proposed by the SEU.[8] Beginning from a critical assumption that social exclusion is constituted locally, the document seeks both to identify the extent and causes of problems of area-based social exclusion and to propose ways of dealing with them. Considerable stress is placed upon the failure of mainstream top-down policies delivered through vertically-organised and rule-bound Whitehall departments, and blighted by short-term 'initiative-itis' and a lack of local co-ordination. It describes what does 'work' via a series of 'best practice' case studies of community-based social economy organisations. Community-based initiatives loom large in this vision of future anti-poverty strategies. The overall direction of the proposed policy programme consists of new area-based initiatives, supported by a 'backdrop' of national policies and firmly based on the development of local community-based social economy organisations. The *National Strategy* 'offers a comprehensive approach to tackling deprivation at the community level' (SEU 2001: 45). National policy thus amounts to the sum of these localised solutions.

The *New Deal for Communities* (hereafter NDC), a £900 million scheme to provide funds for the intensive regeneration of the eighty-eight most deprived local authority districts (SEU 2001: 44) was the first expression of this new philosophy. It was introduced within the *National Strategy* and launched in the same week. The purpose of the NDC programme was to establish local community-led regeneration partnerships in seventeen 'Pathfinder areas' throughout England, followed in 2000 by a further twenty-two. By 2001, thirty-nine neighbourhoods had therefore received funding through the NDC.[9] Furthermore, 'the Government's long-term vision is that in ten to twenty years no-one should be seriously disadvantaged by where they live' (SEU 2001: 45) – an ambitious target given both the contemporary breadth and depth of socio-spatial inequality and the history of uneven development in the UK.

'Genuine' – as opposed to instrumental fund-gaining – partnership is seen as vital to the success of NDC and 'communities are key partners locally' (SEU 2001: 45). The purpose of these 'genuine partnerships' is to 'improve job prospects, bring together investment in buildings and investment in people, and to improve neighbourhood management and the delivery of local services' (DETR 1998: 4). Moreover, 'The new programme will support plans that bring together local people, community and voluntary organisations, public agencies, local authorities and business in an intensive local focus to tackle these problems and make a lasting improvement' (DETR 1998: 1).

The NDC rules require that the area funded should be a 'recognisable neighbourhood'. The explanation of what this might mean in practice is that the neighbourhood:

> . . . should not be so large that the partnership cannot focus its strategy effectively. Nor should it be so small that effective neighbourhood management strategies cannot be put in place. Communities will typically, therefore, be expected to cover between 1000 to 4000 households within a distinct area.
>
> (DETR 1998: 9)

The NDC lays out a range of suggested outputs, some of which would need to form part of successful bids to the programme. These are, in the order they appear in the original documentation (DETR 1998: 6–7): Jobs, Housing, Neighbourhood Management, Enterprise Development, Crime and Drugs, Education, Health, Access to Services, Families, Young People and Children, Access to Information, and Community Building. Whichever of these are prioritised by a partnership, the activities that it undertakes are strictly time-limited. All capital spending within the framework of NDC must take place within the first five years of the programme. Each partnership has an absolute life-span of ten years and is required to submit a 'clear forward strategy which explains how the partnership will keep going beyond this ten year period' (DETR 1998: 13).

The local and neighbourhood focus of NDC and the *National Strategy for Neighbourhood Renewal* is seen as an important policy innovation, allowing customised local solutions to problems of social exclusion. This attaches a great deal of weight to the local level and the efficacy of localised solutions to problems of social exclusion, which even the SEU recognises to be a consequence of economic globalisation and national societal change. The SEU (2001: 25) acknowledges, 'the economic changes that have driven social exclusion include a more open global economy that has meant more competition and the need continually to up-date skills and the growth of knowledge-based industries that require higher levels of qualification'. At the same time, 'communities have become more polarised and fragmented, so that, for example, poor and unemployed people are less likely to live in a community where others might be able to put them in touch with a job'. It is a paradox that the solution proposed is to transfer considerable responsibility to the local level and to local partnerships and communities in abolishing serious disadvantage. In this way, NDC, as part of the national government's overall anti-exclusion programme, is presented as a distinct and positive break from past area-based regeneration projects because of their emphasis on local control and entrepreneurial approaches (Sewel 1998).

Conclusion: the UK in wider context

The Third Way politics of New Labour claims to steer a middle course between an older cross-party consensual 'One Nation' strategy – essentially social democratic – and the subsequent and a more recent and divisive 'Two Nations' strategy, associated above all with the politics of Thatcherism. Despite the rhetorical claims, it is clear that the Third Way is much less of a middle way than a course that owes much more to the Thatcherite politics of 'Two Nations' than it does to the 'One Nation' consensual politics of Macmillan,[10] Heath, and Wilson. It has a distinctly blue rinse. It begins from an assertion that adaptation to global economic forces is the only feasible policy option. Everything else, not least the government's public spending profile and priorities, must be fitted around this. This includes tackling social exclusion, 'one of the key upward pressures on public spending' (SEU 2001: 23). Thus social exclusion must be reduced but equally in ways that make minimal demands upon public expenditure. From this has

followed an emphasis upon individual, neighbourhood, and community responsibility for devising ways of tackling social exclusion via local social economy and
other initiatives. Government financial support for these is available but is strictly
time-limited and short-term and tied to specific and measurable outcomes and
clearly identified exit strategies that do not depend upon continuing public sector
funding. In subsequent chapters we explore these rules and their outcomes in
greater detail.

This inflection is close to a new policy regime in the EU. Issues of the potential
of the social economy and the extent to which, and conditions under which, this
can be realised could become normalised as part of a new modernity. But the
conception of the social economy as a localised solution to localised problems of
social exclusion is not hegemonic yet. We saw in Chapter 1, in fact, other national
models imagine the social economy in a different way. They raise several issues.
First, and contrary to New Labour's position, is the possibility that the social
economy can be made compatible with equitable welfare provision within a
progressive politics of redistribution. This is perhaps most clearly demonstrated
by the position in Scandinavia. Second, there is no necessary reason why the social
economy should be ghettoised and confined to locations of extreme social
exclusion and deprivation. Indeed, to do so may conceal from public view and
exacerbate the extreme social exclusion experienced by marginalised poor people
in affluent areas, for example. Third, it is necessary to be aware of what the social
economy might reasonably be expected to achieve and the optimal arrangements
in which it might realise its full potential:

> There is a tendency, however, for an agenda of difficult tasks to be placed at
> the door of the Social Economy: the creation of employment, the reduction
> of unemployment, the promotion of local development, the reduction of
> poverty and the general improvement in the quality of life – which neither the
> state nor the private sectors, with their vastly superior resources, have been
> able to achieve to date. Communities suffering from poverty and unemploy-
> ment will not successfully deal with these problems on their own.
>
> (Molloy *et al.* 1999)

This is a sobering assessment.

Fourth, defining the social economy as an aggregate of local initiatives
necessarily defines the social economy as fragmented and heterogeneous. While
heterogeneity may represent local flexibility and the capacity to customise local
solutions to local circumstances, variety could become a reason for not tackling
social exclusion to a uniform national standard, as a national problem. It could
even blunt scrutiny of national policies which might be incompatible or in conflict
with the objective of alleviating social exclusion at the local level. The social
economy, and in particular its local discursive constitution, may then be thought
of as part of a new governmentality that seeks to defuse and control proposals for
radical change rather than becoming a conduit for promoting such change.
Indeed, there is evidence of a new governmentality emerging around the social

economy, closely tied to the construction of international data bases that seek to promote 'best practice', such as those of UNESCO and the EU. One important effect of this is to decontextualise local social economy projects, with the effect of writing out specificity, both of project and place, and emphasising those aspects seen as transferable among projects and places. This is becoming the basis of an evolving consensus among international policy communities and a disciplining device for 'non-conforming' welfare models.

The next three chapters examine current practice among existing social economy organisations in the UK. Chapter 3 examines these organisations thematically, in terms of the range of expectations placed upon them within current academic and policy debates. Four main strands of these expectations are identified and considered in the light of detailed empirical evidence on a range of local economy initiatives. The two chapters which follow then consider the nature of the local social economy in two pairs of places to examine the powers of place and some of the place-specific determinants of social economy activity. This will help reveal the variety that exists within the UK, and so the validity of claims that the social economy might provide a solution to problems of social exclusion in all places in the UK.

3 Policy and practice in the UK social economy

Introduction

As we have seen, the social economy is defined in contemporary policy as an agglomeration of local interventions in 'localities', 'communities' and 'neighbourhoods', expected to help overcome social exclusion. More specifically, social enterprises are expected to create employment, be financially independent, succeed through serving local markets, and empower the excluded. The purpose of this chapter is to analyse these expectations, as well as forge new understandings, using data drawn from our UK-wide investigation of local social enterprises. Fuller details of these data sources and our research methodology are given in the Preface and in the Appendix (pp. 126–30).[1]

Employment and training

A central role that the local social economy is expected to play is that of creating new forms of employment in excluded communities. The European Commission (EC), for example, has identified nineteen fields of activity on the basis of which it has proclaimed an 'Era of Tailor Made Jobs' (CEC 1998a).[2] These various activities are echoed in the policy pronouncements of New Labour and other centre-right national governments for whom the local social economy offers the promise of 'bottom-up' regeneration with new sources of employment flowing from the conversion of 'needs into markets'. Social economy organisations contributing to employment outcomes fall into two main categories: direct employers and labour market intermediaries. The direct employers are expected to create jobs by exploiting new areas of anticipated growth. These include, for example, environmental schemes as a basis for socially useful employment (Altvater 1993; Lipietz 1992, 1995), the provision of new and/or alternative social services beyond the state (Gough 1979; Haughton 1998, 1999), and the creation of non-monetary local exchange networks (Ekins 1986, 1992; Ekins and Newby 1998; Offe and Heinze 1992; Lee 1996; Bowring 1998). Labour market intermediaries include organisations developing active labour market policies, such as Intermediate Labour Market training schemes to help the excluded to return to work in the formal economy. In all cases it is additional employment that is expected to be created around needs and markets poorly served at the present.

However, the evidence-base for the capacity of the social economy to create employment is relatively thin. What is known is that a large but often unspecified number of people are employed (including volunteers) in the Third Sector, understood in the broadest sense to encompass not only organisations comprising the social economy but also the full range of voluntary and charitable organisations. Although there is an absence of data providing a reliable estimate of the numbers involved at a national level,[3] there have been isolated attempts to quantify the total numbers employed in the social economy in specific places.

A study carried out by the Territorial Employment Research Unit (TERU) at the University of Glasgow for the Glasgow-based social economy consultants Community Enterprise in Strathclyde in 1996–7, for example, estimated that the social economy in Lowland Scotland employed 42,000 people – as many as the then booming electronics industry in the region (McGregor *et al.* 1997). However, as the TERU also reported, of these 42,000 estimated jobs, only 8300 were held by people from 'disadvantaged areas' and 5800 by people from 'disadvantaged groups' (these figures overlapping to some degree) (ibid.: ii). However, these numbers relate to the social economy defined as the non-profit sector in general, rather than being confined to the 17 per cent of the organisations surveyed that 'fall unambiguously into the community enterprise model' (McGregor *et al.* 1997). This suggests that the actual employment outcomes in areas of the greatest need are in practice quite low, particularly in relation to levels of need.

Elsewhere, a recent audit of the social economy in Bristol carried out in 2000 for the City Council found that the total employment within a self-selecting sample of 404 social economy organisations in the city amounted to over 4700 jobs, of which just over 50 per cent were full-time. In the case of the Bristol audit, considerable criticism has been directed at the statistics by local social economy activists themselves who feel that they misrepresent the situation in important ways. As one prominent local activist put it,

> If I wanted I could interpret these figures to support any project that you would want to propose for funding, and I shouldn't be able to do that. These figures don't tell us very much about what the need is. I have been to most of the meetings at which these things have been discussed and it has been very hard to reach agreement. I am still not clear about all this and I have been through hours of meeting – nothing has moved on in terms of definition.[4]

The majority of the organisations audited in Bristol were not social enterprises as such but a wide variety of different charitable and voluntary organisations. Of the 404 projects included, only 17 per cent were, according to local sources, properly classified as part of the social economy.

While figures such as those for Bristol and Glasgow are open to varying interpretation and criticism, they have not dampened the enthusiasm of policy-makers for the social economy because even this scanty evidence is seen to show that local interventions have the capacity to deliver jobs. Much of this enthusiasm has been built around scattered projects. Let us turn to these experiences to see whether the enthusiasm is justified.

In certain sectors of the social economy, there are indeed areas where employment has been created through organisations taking advantage of new forms of funding or new markets spawning from work previously carried on informally or by local authorities. The care sector is a good example in which innovative forms of service delivery have produced substantial numbers of jobs, often for women. Increasing state funding for childcare services, as part of an attempt to help lone parents into work, has led to the creation of some quite large organisations. Perhaps the biggest of these, One Plus in Glasgow, currently employs 135 permanent staff, 110 intermediate labour market staff, 100 sessional staff and a further 60 people through a jointly-owned subsidiary company. One Plus also provides up to 310 training places at any one time. As the importance of the availability of affordable child-care has become increasingly recognised by both funders and the UK government (particularly since 1997), so similar organisations have developed in other places. Elsewhere in Glasgow, Calton Childcare provides a smaller-scale child-care service employing 65 women from various parts of the East End of the city. In Belfast, several women's projects have developed around the provision of child-care and child-care training for local women, in addition to a range of other social and employment services. The Shankill Women's Centre, for example, has played an important role as an employer and trainer in the conventional sense for local women, providing some 38 full-time jobs (in 1998), and it has helped women to overcome problems associated with sectarianism through education and inter-community dialogue.

Similar growth has been seen in homecare services for the elderly and infirm, which are increasingly being delivered by co-operative social enterprises. The Wrekin Care Co-operative is one of the largest of a number of such organisations throughout the UK, providing work for as many as ninety-five full and part-time carers at any one time. The organisation derives 25 per cent of its income from local authority contracts, and the rest from direct payment by clients. In practice, however, these latter are the attendance allowances paid to clients by the state, then transferred to the co-operative as payments for services rather than to the local health authority.

Although such schemes have created significant numbers of jobs throughout the UK, many of them are displacements from the public sector and they are often short-term and poorly paid. Wrekin Care has suffered from significant fluctuations in the numbers of carers it has on its books, a fact that it attributes to the hard and stressful nature of the job and an hourly rate (in 1999) of just £4.50 per hour (rising to £6 per hour at weekends) for a 20–5- or 40-hour week. In addition, the carers are not employed directly by the co-operative but are self-employed, working on a sessional basis for a number of hours agreed in advance with the co-operative. As self-employed workers, homecare staff have to pay all expenses (including, for example the costs of running a car, which is essential to the work) out of their own pocket. Although these costs can be offset against tax, the jobs created by the co-operative do not offer the same job-security, benefits or support structures that could be expected from formal employment in the public or larger private sector organisations.

Although our study reveals that many of the jobs created by the social economy are low-paid and precarious, there are examples where more secure employment has been generated. Amman Valley Enterprises (AVE), in the former coalfields of South Wales, for example, has created fifty-seven permanent jobs for local people since it was created in 1987. The project was established by a group of local women with funding from the local authority and the EU in the aftermath of the 1984–5 miners' strike and in anticipation of the closure of neighbouring pits in the late 1980s. AVE was a reaction to the increasingly urgent needs of women in the area to gain marketable qualifications in recognition of their increasing importance in the local labour market as wage earners, often the sole wage earner in a household. AVE was initially established purely as a training organisation, but quite early on began to identify aspects of its own activity, particularly catering and computing, that could be established semi-independently of the core business as community enterprises. To date, AVE has established seven different community enterprises, three of which are now run as separate enterprises with a permanent staff.

For the majority of projects in our study, however, the main contribution to local employment has been indirect, usually taking the form either of comprehensive training and advice schemes or supported workspace schemes. While Pecan Ltd in Peckham in South London has created some employment for local people among its own staff, the main impact of the initiative has been through the provision of very flexible and innovative training programmes, tailored to the needs of the local community. It is claimed that Pecan's training courses have made a 'significant' contribution to the reduction of unemployment in the area, by overcoming specific barriers to labour-market access among particular communities. This is especially the case among members of the local Nigerian and Somali communities who have been helped to overcome barriers of language, culture, and lack of basic skills which had previously denied them access to many forms of work. Importantly, however, the employment outcomes of Pecan are not themselves primarily in the social economy. Rather it has improved access to the mainstream labour market, a task made much easier in recent years due to the growth in the London economy overall and in the demand for minimally-skilled labour.

In contrast, where the local labour market is less buoyant, and where the needs of local people are much more acute, the contribution of the social economy to local employment can be very different. Govan Workspace in Glasgow, for example, has protected and created local employment, not in the social economy or through training, but by helping to preserve and protect private sector activity within an area of very low inward investment, blighted by problems of severe deprivation. Govan Workspace owns and manages three units for industrial and small businesses employing over 530 jobs, of which 50 per cent are held by people living in the immediate area. It is unlikely that many of the jobs preserved within the workspace companies would otherwise have arisen in Govan and, indeed, attempts continue to be made to poach Govan-based firms to other parts of the city. The significance of the Workspace project has been to avoid jobs being displaced elsewhere.

Even for the biggest and best known social economy projects in the UK, the outcomes in terms of employment are mixed. The Wise Group, for example, has the reputation of being one of the great success stories of the social economy. While it is a large organisation with over 200 mainly full-time staff, these are often professional and skilled jobs that are rarely accessible to members of Wise's main client group – long-term unemployed people with few skills and little or no work-experience. Wise's main contribution to the local labour market is one of 'churning', providing periodic employment for people with either very few marketable skills or who live in unemployment blackspots. Although a majority of Wise trainees do go on to find paid work, almost 50 per cent of its clients are unemployed three months after leaving the scheme and 44 per cent after six months. This suggests that while Wise provides a very valuable service to the people of Glasgow and beyond (see Chapter 4), this cannot disguise the fact that its contribution to stimulating local labour market demand is minimal. This shows that however successful the social economy might be at providing services, it may in itself not make up for the absence of employment in the mainstream economy.

Another very important element in assessing the effectiveness of the social economy as a means of creating or facilitating employment is that of cost. In practice, costs vary enormously between individual projects. Pecan Ltd, for example, estimates that the cost of passing each client through training and into the labour market (if not directly into work) is around £2000. The Wise Group, by contrast, claims an average cost of £14,100 per client. Taken at face value and without qualification, these figures would seem to represent massive and inexplicable variations in the costs of training and/or job creation. That said, these figures take no account of the differential character of the local labour market, the particular skills and/or experience being imparted, the way in which the client relates to the project or the 'value-added' that the investment represents. The Wise Group, for example, defends the high cost of its service by pointing out that to leave people on benefit costs approximately £8900 per year, without altering their employment prospects. On the other hand, the wages earned by Wise employees support the local economy by generating £2.10 for every £1.00 invested by the Local Authority and yields £7.25 million in tax revenues for the national exchequer. Costs also need to be related to a host of local factors and to the extent to which expenditure circulates with positive multiplier effects within the local economy.

Perhaps the most significant determinant of the costs associated with creating or accessing employment through the social economy is the character and extent of its relationship to the mainstream economy. Costs for Pecan are so low, partly because it tends to deal with a more 'job-ready' clientele, partly because the buoyant London labour market has more than enough capacity to absorb its clients. In the case of Wise, the opposite set of conditions prevail. The Wise client group comprises the long-term unemployed with little or no work experience and therefore require considerably more investment in terms of time and resources to give them access to very limited opportunities in a competitive local labour-market.

Our evidence tends to show that despite the headline figures that are sometimes produced to show that the social economy can combat problems of localised unemployment, its capacity to create significant levels of employment in the places in which it is most needed is typically limited and circumscribed.

Financial independence

Much policy support for the social economy is predicated on the belief that social enterprises can be self-funding in the longer term (CEC 1998a,b) and that they can develop capital assets for the local community (e.g. community-centres, office space, low-rent housing, and so on). The NDC, for example, is quite explicit that it will only consider projects that, 'have a clear forward strategy which explains how the partnership will keep the momentum going beyond [the] ten-year period [of funding]' (DETR 1998: 18). Just as social enterprises are expected to generate employment, they are also expected to develop, therefore, some form of growth market within the areas in which they operate that will generate a trading surplus to replace or offset public funds in the long term.

In practice only a very small number manage to free themselves of grant funding completely. Our analysis of 195 social economy projects across the UK in the period between 1997–2000 shows that 67 per cent were wholly reliant on public funds and a further 21 per cent relied on the public purse for at least 70 per cent of their income (Table 3.1). Only 3 per cent could report that they were wholly free of public sector grants for revenue funding, but even among these projects, some made sporadic use of grants for new project development.

Table 3.1 Grant dependency of UK social economy organisations

Percentage of income from direct grants	Number of organisations (total = 195)
0	6
1–9	4
10–19	3
20–9	4
30–9	2
40–9	2
50–9	2
60–9	5
70–9	4
80–9	15
90–9	17
100	131

Source: figures derived from category searches of the LOCIN database at http://locin.jrc.it

This high level of dependence on public funds is by no means confined to the UK. Analysis of the 723 social economy organisations included in the EC's LOCIN database reveals that 482 (67 per cent) cited their local government authority as a source of some or all funding and 398 (55 per cent) stated that their national government funded their activity. By contrast only 26 (4 per cent) of these projects could state that they were wholly independent of external funding sources. [The organisation of the information within this database prevents the production of more detailed aggregate break-downs of the financial independence of these projects.] Since a basic criterion for inclusion in the LOCIN database was that projects must have been established for at least three years, this level of dependence cannot simply be attributed to the newness of social economy activity. Of course, independence does not necessarily imply that projects must become wholly self-financing. For example, it can be defined as moving to a balancing of sources of income such that the proportion of grant income tends to fall over time, leaving grant income to be used to best effect overall. However, in the context of falling welfare budgets, it may well be that the financial autonomy expected of the social economy will become simply a substitute for state welfare expenditure rather than a genuine addition to the resources available for tackling poverty and exclusion.

Within the general picture that a very limited number of projects are in any way financially autonomous, there are none the less important examples in which innovative development strategies, creative use of public sector sources and often fortuitous local conditions have enabled social economy projects to develop significant income streams and assets. The Furniture Resource Centre Ltd (FRC), for example, has grown from being a small furniture recycling organisation to designing, manufacturing, and marketing its own furniture. FRC was established by evangelical Christians in 1988 in a warehouse in Speke on Merseyside with the help of a Church Urban Fund donation. The original purpose of FRC was to help resolve a chronic problem of inadequate furniture and domestic equipment in the available social housing, often resulting in a very high turnover of social housing among some of the most vulnerable groups. FRC started off by providing low-cost recycled furniture to such people, but from 1994, it established a production unit in addition to its recycling workshop. The unit produces high-quality, low-cost new furniture for sale to people on low incomes or to social landlords through the national Furnished Homes Scheme. It has developed a range of products which are either sold directly to people in social housing or, increasingly, to local authorities and housing associations as 'furniture packs' containing the necessary items to make housing habitable. From the outset one of the central aims of the project was to develop a range of activities that would generate an income and allow it to operate independently of the vagaries of public funding regimes. Although project leaders report considerable difficulties over the years in achieving this level of independence, by 1998 over 90 per cent of FRC's £4 million annual turnover was derived from sales of products – both its own manufactures and recycled furniture and white goods. While much of FRC's income is still ultimately derived from the public sector (though increasingly from private and Third Sector Registered Social Landlords), it is in the form of payment for goods and services provided, rather than as grants or via service level contracts. FRC has been able to develop a niche market to exploit the considerable sums spent on social housing on Merseyside, to provide a valuable social service – turnover rates on social housing have fallen – as well as a viable and independent social enterprise.

In other cases, projects have been created specifically to manage and further develop existing assets. For example, Coin Street Community Builders (CSCB) on the south bank of the Thames was established to act as a management and development company for a 14-acre site, after the local community won a long campaign to prevent the area being sold to commercial developers for office buildings. The Greater London Council sold the site to CSCB for a fraction of its market value and protected its status as a community-owned asset through a series of binding covenants. The result has been the creation of a varied development scheme embracing tenant-owned and managed social housing schemes, work-spaces for private sector designers, retail outlets and catering, exhibition spaces, public parks, training and employment services, and an annual community arts festival. These activities provide CSCB with the revenue to grow as an independent organisation.

While the number of projects that have survived independently of public sector funding is limited, other examples reveal that relatively low levels of additional finance for marginal innovations can have a significant impact. The Matson Neighbourhood Project (MNP) is based in a housing estate on the outskirts of Gloucester and has been particularly effective in using its activities for wider community benefit. For example, once, in conducting an estate-wide survey of residents, £1 was paid for each survey form completed in order to ensure the fullest return possible. Instead of using the project office as the collection point, a local chemist facing closure due to lack of business, was used to gather the forms and handle the payments. The result of simply bringing people through the doors of the chemist had an immediate positive impact on trade, effectively saving the business. MNP was also instrumental in saving a greengrocer's shop in the main shopping parade on the estate which was due to close because the disabled owner could no longer afford the rent or manage the floorspace. MNP took over the lease of the shop for one of its advice centres, allowing the grocer to move to smaller, cheaper premises next door. Since the move, business has increased considerably again saving the shop and the livelihood of the owner.

By bringing commercial and social enterprises together and creating complementary services MNP has been very effective in developing an enhanced level of economic activity on the estate. Income from both grant sources and from commercial activities remains in circulation in the immediate area and helps prevent further local economic decline. There are also clear social benefits to the preservation and creation of local shops and services. However, for all its success in stimulating a certain, albeit low, level of economic activity, MNP remains heavily reliant on grant income and is unlikely to become self-financing in the foreseeable future. In total, MNP is able to generate 15 per cent of its income through the sale of services, most of which is derived from service level agreements with the local health trust. The remainder comes from the local authority, the National Lotteries Charities Board, private sector sponsorship and a range of small, one-off grants.

For the bulk of the social economy, the major source of income remains the public sector, either directly in the form of grants or indirectly through service contracts. Often this dependency is an obstacle to change. Some funders, for example, claw back surplus funds at the end of the funding period (SEL 2000). Not only are funders notoriously 'risk averse', but many are formally prevented from funding any organisation that explicitly intends to generate a surplus. National Lottery funds, for example, cannot be used to support social enterprises which are established to create a surplus, even though it is not distributed as profit (SEL 2000). The availability of most funds on only an annual cycle, changing criteria for eligibility, onerous administrative and supervision requirements, and a host of particular problems (such as retrospective and often late payment by the European Social Fund) makes medium to long-term financial planning impossible. Such constraints raise the prospect that what is being created are, in effect, 'ghetto economies' which can do little more than ensure the short-term recirculation of grant funding and the limited disposable income available to local people. This, of course, in many instances does represent an improvement in the day-to-day economic lives of people living in deprived communities. However, without changes in the structure of current funding arrangements to permit longer-term planning and the accumulation of community-owned capital, the social economy offers few prospects for becoming financially independent, and using this independence to develop needed new services.

Success through local markets?

Social enterprises are routinely understood to operate at a local scale to meet very specific local needs through the mobilisation of local capacities. The assumption is that a local circuitry of need and response will spawn viable social enterprises. Our evidence questions this assumption. Local focus in practice can prove to be a limiting factor on growth by restricting the level and character of demand for the goods and services provided. Conversely, there are many examples of apparently successful projects where the connections to small bounded neighbourhoods are either tenuous or non-existent. These contradictions highlight a potential tension between meeting local needs and being dragged down by responding to local demand alone.

In South Wales, for example, there is a cluster of social economy projects in the valleys of the former coalfield, most of which have established some form of community enterprise using national (both UK government and the recently established Welsh Assembly) and European funds. The range of activities among them is quite narrow, consisting for the most part of semi-industrial potteries, carpentry workshops, furniture exchanges, catering, garden centres, and landscaping services. All of these activities are conducted on a very small scale, reflecting their primary objective of providing jobs and services within the immediate neighbourhood. While some of these enterprises are successful as micro ventures, their capacity for expansion or diversification is limited. They saturate the local market with similar products, and local labour markets can only absorb so many people being trained in the same skills, which are often unrelated to the demands of the mainstream formal labour-market. The same limited range of activities serve the same set of local needs and chase the same limited local disposable income. The restriction on spending power further limits the possibilities of diversifying into 'new' products and services. Despite exhortations on the part of community sector umbrella organisations that local initiatives should seek to break out of their immediate local areas, very little is done in practice to overcome the inherent limitations of the activities pursued (West 1999). However, were they to do so, the character of the local connections would change, perhaps in ways that would run counter to the prevailing criteria for funding, so that 'delocalisation' might create problems of its own.

Some of the larger and better established social enterprises in the UK have been able to sidestep such limitations by operating on much bigger and/or multiple scales. Although often still described as 'local', such organisations are effectively detached from any identifiable area or community, sometimes operating up to and including the national level. Perhaps the clearest example of this is the Wise Group which is routinely cited as an exemplar of best practice in the 'local' social economy (see, for example, CEC 1998a,b; SEU 1998). In practice, however, Wise was oriented towards local neighbourhoods only for a short time in the early 1980s. When it began, the project's services (insulation, security devices, and landscaping in areas of social housing combined with training) were delivered by community-based 'squads' scattered throughout Glasgow and responsible for particular areas and/or communities. As the project has grown, however, the organisation of the Wise intermediate labour market in Glasgow has been organised on a city-wide basis, with all operations based in the project's Charlotte Street offices. In addition, Wise has developed a number of subsidiaries and associated projects in cities throughout the UK which, although more or less local depending on the nature of the local labour market, follow a model developed elsewhere. Since its inception, Wise has followed its chairman's oft-stated belief that if something is to be effective it has to be done 'at scale'. More recently, following changes in the nature of employment services and Scottish devolution, Wise has taken on an increasingly regional and even national role. Not only has Wise bid to run one of the government's pilot regional Single Work Access Gateways (Clyde Coast), but it is also looking to expand further as a provider of training and work-experience throughout the UK.

The ability to work beyond the local market has also contributed to the economic and political success of other projects. The Furniture Resource Centre has been able to become financially independent in large part because of the wide social housing market that it has been able to tap into throughout Merseyside and, increasingly, the rest of England. Without access to a market on this scale, the project would not have been able to grow or to diversify into other forms of social provision, recycling, training, and manufacturing. Indeed the reputation of the organisation on a local and regional scale has also allowed it to contribute to national debates, for example, through evidence to policy committees and by research demonstrating the need for reforms to housing policy (Frances 1988; *Financial Times* 1998).

Similarly, Coin Street Community Builders has been successful precisely because its location in central London has allowed it to transcend the limitations of local demand alone. As Coin Street has developed local housing co-operatives, so increasing amounts of private housing have been developed on adjoining sites attracted by the infrastructural and environmental improvements created by the project. By targeting its workspaces at the particular niche market of young creative designers, Coin Street has been able to bring in a range of industries that together constitute a considerable change in the nature of the local economy. More importantly, perhaps, the concentration of designers within one of the project's main building, the Oxo Tower, has attracted further numbers of designers, artists, and their various customers and collectors to an area that they would previously have avoided. By encouraging the development of both small cafeterias and bistros, as well as an internationally-renowned restaurant, Coin Street has been able to exploit the presence of large numbers of people working in local businesses and, increasingly, tourists and bon-viveurs from throughout London and beyond.

The localness exhibited by Coin Street is of a particular kind. Local services have been created for local people, but the resources marshalled to make this happen have not been exclusively those of local people. Rather, Coin Street has been able fundamentally to alter the boundaries of the local economy by breaking down economic, social, and political barriers that previously isolated this particular part of the inner-city from the rest of London. Prior to the development of the Coin Street site, the local economy was in sharp decline following the demise of the London Docks upon which many local businesses – primarily warehouses and processing plants – had depended. The local population was also falling, partly because of a lack of local employment and partly because social housing in the area was among the worst in London. It has only been by addressing these severe limitations of the local area, not least by connecting it to the wider political economy of London, that conditions have been put in place that have allowed the creation of a successful social enterprise and the regeneration of the area. Of course this was greatly helped by the fact that Coin Street is situated within the wealthy and complex economy of London. As a result, the process of 'reconnection' has been very much easier than it would have been in more physically isolated communities. Coin Street's major contribution to the local area has, therefore, not so much been the mobilisation and preservation of localness, but the careful management of its transition from a place isolated by poverty and poor housing to an integrated part of the wider economy while respecting the needs and aspirations of the existing population.

Although widely seen as a *sine qua non* of social economy success, the significance of localness is therefore ambiguous for a number of reasons. First, the degree to which social enterprises relate to the local areas that they are intended to serve varies enormously, ranging between identifiable and self-defining communities up to city and region-wide catchments. In some cases the 'community' served may be a specific interest group (youth, the homeless, the learning disabled, for example) rather than a single, territorially-defined population. In other words, although all social economy organisations are expected to be local, some are considerably more local than others and local may not be defined spatially but in terms of other shared interests.

Second, the extent to which the 'localness' of the social economy is a product of local factors (e.g. local needs identified and acted upon by local people), rather than the exigencies of regional or national policy programmes, is neither always evident nor obvious. While the social economy is expected to tap into and/or constitute some form of 'authentic' local capacity as the basis for the alternative it offers, the prescriptive nature of much public policy might suggest another reading. If a community focus arises more out of the demands and expectations of national policy than from existing structures and capacities in local communities, to what extent can this be said to be local?

Third, this is particularly significant in relation to the ways in which the social economy is seen to provide a local 'alternative' to mainstream economic practice and welfare provision. Specifically it is important to make a careful distinction between 'local' as a site at which alterity is developed and expressed and the presentation of the 'local' as the alternative itself. If the local is the site at which alterity is expressed, as is certainly the case of projects such as the CSCB and MNP, then the nature of the local is fluid and inclusive. The significance of locality for these projects is not that it delineates and defines a single bounded space within which social economy activities are contained (the local can refer as much to a city as a neighbourhood), but defines a point of commonality that serves to unite people as local. The local community in such circumstances effectively becomes an alternative centre (alternative to, for example, a local authority or an entrenched political establishment) around which other activities develop. In the notion that locality *is* the alternative, however, the nature of the 'local' is more problematic. Where the local scale is promoted as the appropriate alternative scale for welfare provision and alternative employment creation, then it is accompanied by issues about where local boundaries begin and end. It is for this reason that, as welfare policy has come increasingly to embrace the local as the appropriate site of intervention, considerable efforts have been made to quantify local spaces. For example, in the UK, the Centre for the Analysis of Social Exclusion (CASE) at the London School of Economics, which was established in 1997, has worked closely with the Social Exclusion Unit in defining localised welfare areas, often prescribing community-based social economy solutions (see, for example, Smith 1999; Glennerster *et al.* 1999; Power and Bergin 1999). In this version, though, the issue of whether the local as a bounded space can provide the requisite level of social capacity and demand for goods and services, remains unproblematised.

Empowerment

Although the concept of empowerment is often used by Third Sector activists in relation to the social economy, the extent to which empowerment is achieved in practice varies enormously. There are examples of projects that have been able to meet the objectives of business plans drawn up with funders while forcing open previously closed and often hostile political structures to the scrutiny and control of local people. There are also examples of projects that have been in existence for as long as thirty years, and have been considered as examples of best practice, which have effectively excluded local people from such decision-making processes in ways that are profoundly disempowering rather than empowering.

One of the more positive examples, the Matson Neighbourhood Project, provides a particularly striking example of local empowerment. The project was founded after a successful campaign to prevent the local housing estate being sold off to a private housing association by the local authority. The campaign was successful because the founders of MNP were able to mobilise local residents, with the help of both the local Labour and Liberal Democrat parties, to remove the ruling Conservative group from Gloucester City Council through a highly organised form of tactical voting. The Liberal Democrats, who succeeded the Conservatives in the Council, recognised the central role played by the Matson campaign by overturning the sell-off plans and giving their active support to the neighbourhood project. Although MNP has not subsequently deployed this form of direct democracy, the knowledge among residents (not to mention the Council) that electoral action can yield significant results has transformed the local political environment. Over and above the range of services that MNP has managed to bring onto the estate and the jobs that have been created, the project leaders stress the renewed confidence and sense of community on the estate. This confidence builds on the prior political process in which local people found themselves involved for the first time. The success of MNP in meeting the formal outputs required of the social economy, therefore, is a product of, and in addition to, a much more fundamental and much less quantifiable change in the nature of the local political and social participation. Interestingly, although MNP is cited as an example of best practice by the Social Exclusion Unit in its *National Strategy for Neighbourhood Renewal* (see Chapter 2), no mention is made of the way in which the project came into existence.

A similar silence pervades accounts of an increasingly well-known project, the Arts Factory, based in the South Wales town of Ferndale. Like MNP, part of the Arts Factory's success must be attributed to its capacity to mobilise a largely lethargic local political culture. Rather than achieving this through tactical voting, however, the Arts Factory earned the support of local people after it challenged the local authority over planning applications which would have resulted in the demolition of a Grade 2 listed chapel in the centre of the town. Despite stiff opposition from the local authority, the Arts Factory won the case and control of the building in question which has subsequently been converted into a multi-purpose community centre and social enterprise in its own right. As in the case of

MNP, however, the Arts Factory is far better known for the range of social enterprises that it has established in and around Ferndale (which include a pottery, a carpentry workshop, a landscape art firm, and various youth projects), all of which have created jobs and/or training places for local people. While these various enterprises have indeed been successful, at least part of that success must be attributed to the transformation of the local political climate whereby the social economy organisation has also adopted a strongly political role, altering the relationship between local people and a remote and bureaucratic state. Part of the reason for the peculiar silences surrounding these aspects of the work of MNP, the Arts Factory, and various Northern Irish Women's Projects (see Greencastle Women's Group below) seems to be because power has essentially been taken from the local authority by local people with the help of social entrepreneurs. The Arts Factory operates largely beyond the remit of the local council and often in conflict with it. MNP exists in large part because it has demonstrated the capacity of residents to make or break the controlling group on Gloucester City Council. The Belfast-based Women into Politics project, along with many other women's organisations in the province, has deliberately encouraged women previously ignored by and excluded from the political establishment to take control of their own affairs and to lobby for change. In all three cases, the active transfer of a degree of power over decision-making and resource allocation has been a pre-requisite for the subsequent development of other social and economic outputs. In current social economy policy discourse such democratisation is expected to be the product of these outputs.

In many cases the emphasis on measurable outputs on the part of funders and local authorities has forced initiatives to 'shop-front' activities with output figures to conceal or play down the significance of other achievements and values. When the Spitalfields Small Business Association (SSBA) was established in Tower Hamlets in 1979, for example, project leaders had no intention of creating a small business development unit. On the contrary, their intention was to improve the local housing stock for the Bengali community. However, in order to access funds to launch the project, its leaders realised that they would have to adopt the entrepreneurial language of the time (SSBA was established shortly after Margaret Thatcher came to power). The adoption of the epithet 'small business', was made in recognition of the fact that at that time regeneration funds were being targeted at private sector small and medium enterprise (SME) development and growth. It was only as SSBA grew, and found itself managing a large number of small industrial units containing small businesses (which it had taken over along with the housing above them) that it finally came to conform to its own name. The adoption of the name was not merely opportunistic, however, since the founders of the project were strongly politically opposed to the Thatcherite agenda and quite deliberately sought to appropriate its language to their own ends as a way of subverting that agenda. In this particular case, empowerment involved not simply supporting an isolated and embattled ethnic minority community, but challenging the prevailing Thatcherite national political–economic ideology.

The examples given above are intended to demonstrate that wider, softer forms of empowerment are common goals of social economy activities. Indeed to a large extent this aspect of the social economy is taken for granted by practitioners, however much funders may focus on the quantitative outputs. That said, it would be wrong to suggest that social economy activities always or inevitably produce such outcomes. The social economy certainly does not have the ability automatically to develop this local capacity and to develop structures of local empowerment. One of the longest established social economy projects in the UK, the Craigmillar Festival Society (CFS, founded in the early 1960s), despite being run largely by local people, has been recently found to have largely sidelined and ignored those local residents it was established to support. A recent report commissioned by the City of Edinburgh Council into the thirty-seven community projects working in Craigmillar concluded that:

> the role of the CFS as the 'voice of the people' should be challenged. The perception was that the attendees at the general meetings by which the CFS executive asserted their democratic mandate were generally project staff who had a vested interest in maintaining the status quo.
>
> (DTZ Pieda Consulting 1999: 65)

The status quo consisted, to a large extent, of the 'community'-owned initiative failing to involve the community of Craigmillar and Greater Niddrie in any decisions over the needs and priorities of the local area. As a consequence of this Report, the umbrella organisation for the many community projects operating in the area was dissolved on suspicion of misappropriation of funds and the remaining projects, including CFS, were rationalised and subject to funding cuts. The scale of the problems facing the Craigmillar area were such that regeneration based largely or wholly upon the mobilisation of local capacity, was never going to be easy. Project leaders noted, for example, that anyone who could get a job with the project's help would almost immediately move out of the area, only to be replaced by someone else without work or facing some other range of social problems. However, in the case of CFS, which has long been considered as one of the success stories of the social economy, the project notably failed to develop any alternative social, political or economic structure for local people. The result was pervasive mistrust among local residents who felt, rightly or wrongly, that project leaders were more concerned to develop their own powerbases in the area than to address the needs of the people living there.

In the case of the Paisley Partnership located on the outskirts of Glasgow, repeated attempts to establish social enterprises of various kinds have served, if anything, to further alienate local residents from regeneration activities. The Ferguslie Park Estate, which is the main focus of the partnership, has been the subject of community-based development projects since the late 1960s starting with one of the first Community Development Projects (CDP Inter-Project Editorial Team 1977). Subsequently, for over thirty years, the estate has been the site of various manifestations of community business, area-based partnerships and, most recently, the Social Inclusion Partnership programme.[5] Over time the failure of these successive projects to represent the local people (in similar ways to CFS, for example) or to achieve positive outcomes for local residents (for instance, the community-owned security business was closed after it was discovered to have been running a protection racket) has, if anything, disempowered local people. As different styles and structures of projects have been established in pursuit of different aims, so different local interests have been privileged, represented and/or sidelined. Relations with local residents have progressively deteriorated as factional interests have developed and as project leaders – who in the case of the current partnership are not local residents but professional social entrepreneurs – have found them ever more obstructive. In the Paisley example, the residents' committee, which is represented on the board, is effectively ignored by project leaders, exasperated by demands for services and activities that cannot or can no longer be funded.

Cases such as those of Paisley and Craigmillar provide important lessons for advocates of the more naïve constructions of community-based regeneration. Although empowerment is undoubtedly possible, it cannot simply be assumed to follow from the imposition of a social economy 'model'. In fact, empowerment may be a prerequisite for regeneration rather than a consequence of it. We might suggest, therefore, that the more successful of these examples represent not simply a local 'social economy' but a civic politics through which people are allowed and encouraged to challenge those structures and processes that have produced local exclusion. This, however, is a fundamentally different reading of the social economy than that which currently dominates the policy agenda. Most importantly, it is one that emphasises the capacity of some organisations to counter the *causes* rather than merely the *symptoms* of poverty and marginalisation. In light of this, it is hard to see how economistic conceptions (such as that promoted by the *New Deal for Communities*) can serve as a foundation for meaningful local empowerment. Rather, by propping up the existing social and economic structures of poor places, not least by making assumptions about capacities allegedly latent in the 'local economy', current social economy development policy may unwittingly be reinforcing rather than resolving the problem.

An alternative role: capacity-building and advocacy

The extent to which the social economy has the capacity to deliver the key objectives sought by the mainstream policy community is, therefore, at best ambiguous. As a replacement for provision through the mainstream public or private sectors, the social economy, particularly in those areas of greatest need, has only limited capacity to deliver the levels of service, employment, and empowerment expected by the policy-makers. Our research suggests that in practice, however, the achievements stressed by many successful social economy organisations themselves tend to differ in important respects from those emphasised in the policy literature. While they do indeed stress the importance of creating employment, it is rarely a major aim, not least because they often recognise the limitations of local labour markets on both the supply and demand sides. While most of the projects involved cite sustainability as a primary aim, they usually mean much more than the financial independence which is all too often what the term has come to denote for the policy community. While many social economy organisations stress the importance of delivering services locally and flexibly, the local (the community or the neighbourhood) is not necessarily considered as an end in itself. Instead, a common alternative motif has been advocacy for the principles of *socialised* economic activity, that is, of the desirability of economic involvement to enhance life-chances and the potential for self-development. More specifically, in many cases, existing social economy organisations have been able to demonstrate, again above and beyond the more usual concrete outputs, a contribution to building the capacity of individuals for self-realisation. In this sense, individual capacity is not necessarily concerned with changing the material wealth of the individual, or with enhancing their particular skills, or moving them nearer to the labour market of the formal economy (though it may entail all of these things). Capacity-building is, instead, a question of changing the individual's perception of her or his own life and its possibilities.

Although much of the evidence for this type of capacity-building is inevitably anecdotal, there are a number of projects that include precisely this form of capacity-building as a primary aim and output. Perhaps the most striking of these, if only because of the unique way in which it has been able to demonstrate it in practice, is the Greencastle Women's Group in north Belfast. The project is situated on a predominantly Catholic housing estate that lacked basic amenities and was largely cut off from the surrounding area by a motorway slip-road with no safe crossing. Since the Group was established, housing has been improved, road crossings have been built, jobs have been created through the establishment of child-care facilities on the estate, and the group has begun to generate an income. Indeed it has more than exceeded all of the quantitative targets set by its various funders. The most fundamental change has been, however, in the outlook of the women living on the estate and participating in the project. This is illustrated by two videos in which local women are interviewed; one at the beginning of the project, the other three years later. In the first video many of the women are very bitter about their situation, predominantly talking as victims of the 'troubles', of bureaucratic indifference, and of active discrimination. In the second, the same women are positive, forward-looking and clearly in charge of their own destiny, having thrown off much of the language of sectarianism and having actively worked with the Group to gain qualifications, jobs, and access to decision-makers. The transformation of the lives of individual women in Green-castle will not, in itself, overcome the sectarian problems of the area nor the lack of employment and general poverty. It has, however, produced a form of political dialogue within certain sections of the community, particularly local women. This has resulted in these women acquiring the ability to project a different version of themselves and their community to the outside world in ways in which they quite deliberately reproduce their 'life narratives' (Lash 1994).

Although the process of empowerment is directly evident in the Greencastle videos, in other projects it can be expressed in more subtle and liminal ways. The Third Wave Centre in Derby is a multi-faceted social enterprise developed by a group of committed evangelical Christians over a number of years and providing a range of services for local people. These include a construction training project, a local shop, an employment advice and training centre, a young persons' foyer project, and so on, all run as social enterprises semi-independently of the core organisation. Third Wave has, like Greencastle, been able to meet and exceed all of its output targets and works successfully with all sections of the local community (including, for example, helping to build the local mosque). When we asked how he gauged the success of the project overall, however, the Chief Executive of Third Wave cited the example of a middle-aged woman living in a neighbouring street who, despite having no direct contact with Third Wave, had told her friends that its presence made her feel better about her community. This may not constitute capacity-building in any conventional sense, since the individual in question clearly was not having her access to the labour market improved by Third Wave. Despite this, it was precisely this sort of effect on the surrounding neighbourhood that was taken by the project leader as the most telling evidence of the project's success.

Another example is the Gabalfa Community Workshop in Cardiff, which operates four inter-linked social enterprises that provide employment and training for people with severe learning disabilities. The project runs a carpentry workshop, a café, a garden centre, a pottery, and a gallery/shop, all of which are staffed by people with learning disabilities supervised by professional care workers and trainers. Although the primary aim of Gabalfa has been to create a sustainable way of providing high-quality employment training for groups that were previously denied access to any form of work training, it has done so with a broader aim in mind. By opening retail outlets selling garden centre and pottery products and food direct to the public in competition with other, private sector retailers, Gabalfa has quite deliberately sought to change attitudes towards disabled people among the wider community. By bringing disabled and non-disabled people together in everyday commercial transactions the project has successfully broken though barriers of fear and prejudice on both sides by 'normalising' the presence of disabled in the community.

In all of these cases, success is predicated on the enhancement of the developmental capacities, broadly defined, of specific groups and /or individuals. All of the projects cited above start from the observation that real power derives from access to the requisite social and cultural capabilities. The recent reassertion by Prime Minister Blair that, 'the Government does not accept that the main cause of unemployment and high benefit receipt is a lack of available jobs' (SEU 2001: 69) misses this point. There is also a social geography to exclusion which derives from the unevenly distributed capacity of people to engage in any form of social involvement whether in the workplace or in the wider context of social life as a whole. The development of such capabilities clearly involves the opening up of spaces of reflexive self-constitution to the excluded, but also, importantly, as the case of Gabalfa illustrates, a process of wider advocacy in society at large.

Conclusion

Manifestly, the social economy considered as a varied set of experiences and as a sphere of capability enhancement cannot be reduced to a question of material inputs (resources invested) relative to (short-term) hard outputs (such as numbers of jobs, training places, or national vocational qualifications (NVQs)). Nor can it be confined to a specific geographic or demographic area. Rather, the contribution that the social economy can make to community sustainability depends on a complex range of factors. Some of these factors are already present in the locality and its population, some are created out of local and non-local institutional systems and structures, and some can be developed through the particular form that Third Sector intervention takes. The variety of ways in which the effects of these processes is currently articulated through Third Sector practice in the UK and elsewhere suggests that the institutional form of the social economy for a given community (local or otherwise) cannot be wholly prescribed a priori but emerges over time as part of an evolutionary process. In the case of FRC in Liverpool, for instance, the project's main source of growth was stimulated in part by a legal constraint placed on its existing activities combined with a entrepreneurial capacity on the part of project leaders. MNP and the Arts Factory are both products of political battles out of which local issues and needs were identified and around which local people mobilised. In the cases of Gabalfa and Greencastle Women's Group, the capacity of the individuals in question was enhanced by opening up and giving them access (in the form of both resources and capacities) to other socio-spatial scales. As this implies, developing a relevant social economy organisation does not mean simply consolidating local structures and improving local access to labour markets. Simultaneously it must allow people, individually and collectively, to transcend the limitations and constraints of place. As such it entails (re)creating multi-scalar capacities, infrastructures and connections which allow for the kinds of communication, interaction, and dialogue between social actors at all levels through which civic power is actively reproduced.

That said, the capacities that need to be built, the networks that need to be connected and the forms of empowerment relevant to particular communities will necessarily depend on prevailing conditions and structures. The nature of the problems addressed by the social economy among the women of the Bawnmore estate in Belfast is different from that of Gabalfa's trainees in Cardiff. This is not simply because they constitute different types of 'need community' but because the nature of the social environment that they inhabit and the range of barriers separating them from full participation in it differ. This implies that, while the capacity of social economy organisations to intermediate may well enhance the capacity of poor and marginalized people to produce their own 'life-narratives' (Lash 1994), it can only do so within the constraints of context. In other words, the social economy may well enhance individual capacity, community empowerment and sustainability, but can only do so in direct relation to the distribution of needs, capacities, opportunities, and constraints that exist in particular geographical and social settings. This implies that the effectiveness of social economy organisations in delivering hard or soft outcomes of the type illustrated above will vary. The Third Sector may give people access to their own life-narratives but not necessarily under conditions of their own choosing.

For all its variety and flexibility, the range of organisations that the Third Sector can produce is limited – by funding regimes, by political agendas, by available personnel, by limits to legal forms, and so on. Significantly, this suggests that although local social economy organisations can be seen to produce positive outcomes in terms of both the hard and soft outputs, as illustrated above, they may not be equally relevant to all poor and marginalised communities or people. In other words, and contrary to the assumption prevalent in the current 'best practice' driven policy agenda that successful examples of the local social economy can be used to develop universally applicable models (cf. SEU 1998; DETR 1998; CEC 1998a,b), the factors that allow the social economy to 'succeed' in particular places seem to be quite specific. This suggests that place might matter in the case of the social economy because it seems that the nature of the locality in which it operates is of considerable significance in determining what succeeds and what fails and, for that matter, what success or failure might mean in different local contexts. The influence of the powers of place in shaping the social economy is, however, a dimension that is either wholly absent from conventional particularist academic and policy accounts of the social economy, or which is glossed over in pursuit of some generalisable best practice model. The following two chapters will examine the nature of social economy organisations in four locations of the UK to tease out the significance of place.

4 The corporatist social economy
Glasgow and Middlesbrough

Introduction

The nature of local dynamics may significantly influence social economy outcomes in particular towns, cities, and/or regions in the UK. This observation, relating to the varied abilities of places to combat social exclusion through the social economy, seems submerged in the government's emphasis that all places can respond in similar ways. This is partly due to the government's belief that: 'Governments cannot do this [regeneration] on our own. Indeed it is a mistake to try. But we can help create the economic and social conditions that help communities to help themselves' (Blair 2001).

There is a tacit assumption in a policy programme which has been quite explicitly proposed as a '*national* strategy for *neighbourhood* renewal' that it is possible to deliver national solutions at a local scale. Put another way, the problems faced by deprived communities in the UK are sufficiently similar to be amenable to centrally-devised regeneration schemes delivered through flexible local partnerships and other organisations. Specifically with regard to the social economy component of such policies, there is an assumption that all places, albeit in different ways, possess latent capacities (in terms of social capital, institutional form and/or innovation, and individuals and groups with a strong personal commitment to community) to be able to deliver the kinds of sustainable, responsive, and locally-empowering social enterprises that policy-makers assume is possible. This assumption tends to rest on the understanding that the mechanisms that have generated the various examples of 'best practice' upon which its policy is based, are common to all poor communities. There is assumed to be sufficient commonality in the diversity of powers of place to make such an approach feasible. However, while best practice studies can tell us much about what works in particular places, they also can have the effect of abstracting them from the specific conditions – local, regional and national – in which they have developed and on which they are causally dependent. It may therefore be that it is the specificities – not the commonalites – of the powers of place that are decisive and these may exercise negative as well as positive influences on the character and development of the social economy.

Chapters 4 and 5 examine the relationships between social enterprises and their local contexts – historical, social, and institutional. These two chapters highlight the resulting variety, and also prepare the ground for a discussion in Chapter 6 on the ways in which local context affects the potential of the social economy. We demonstrate through an examination of two 'paired' analyses of four UK urban areas, that the assumption that the social economy is necessarily equally relevant to all local excluded communities is problematic. This chapter compares the way in which the social economy has developed in two places – Glasgow and Middlesbrough – where problems of poverty and exclusion associated with long-term deindustrialisation and a corporatist legacy of governance have shaped a social economy with limited community participation. Chapter 5 compares two places – Bristol and the London Borough of Tower Hamlets – where the problems generated by industrial change and unemployment, but also accompanied by other forms of exclusion (e.g. minority communities surrounded by areas of considerable wealth and prosperity) are associated with a different sort of social economy. These chapters reveal the influence on the local social economy of the historical balance in each place between four variables: the nature and practices of the local state, opportunity in the mainstream economy, the nature of local civil society, and non-local connections offering opportunities for local Third Sector activities. Thus, in each chapter, our paired comparisons of the social economy are prefaced by an account of the economic trends and nature of social exclusion in each urban context, and a summary of local civic and political legacies.

Economic trends and social exclusion

Although the problems facing both Glasgow and Middlesbrough stem from the loss of their respective former industrial bases, the nature and scale of their loss, and the consequences of it, have been different. This is in part due to the period over which the dismantling of the old industrial economy took place. In Glasgow, the mass-employing industries of ship-building, steel-making and other associated manufacturing have been in steady decline since at least the First World War – a secular decline only temporarily delayed by the war economy and the post-war boom (Pacione 1995). For Middlesbrough, the collapse of the local employment base has been more recent, because of repeated waves of investment in Teesside, initially in steel-making and related ship-building and engineering industries, then in the burgeoning inter-war chemicals industry, and subsequently in the post-war chemicals and steel industries. Following the oil crises of the early 1970s and the subsequent rapid restructuring and internationalisation of the chemical and steel making and using industries, however, Teesside experienced rapidly rising unemployment and a general and ongoing disinvestment on the part of those firms that had created and sustained the area over the previous century. Unemployment began to rise steadily in the 1970s and to a rate consistently higher than the national average, peaking at 22–3 per cent in 1984 and 1985 for Cleveland County as a whole, with parts of the inner-urban areas including Middlesbrough reaching 40 per cent (Beynon *et al.* 1994: 105).

As a consequence of the loss of heavy manufacturing capacity and employment, both places have been forced to seek to restructure and diversify their local economies by attracting renewed investment and replacing the employment base. For both, fortunes have been mixed. In Glasgow, while attempts to rekindle manufacturing through heavy investment from the late 1950s in the car and steel industries at Cambuslang, Ravenscraig, and Linwood ultimately failed, considerable numbers of jobs were created in the electronics and services sectors. The electronics industry in Lowland Scotland as a whole currently accounts for around 40,000 jobs. Importantly, however, many of these jobs are located in plants outside of the main conurbation of Glasgow itself – in the so-called 'silicon glen' to the north-west of the city – and did not employ those laid off by the older manufacturing industries.[1]

Much the same is also true of the services sector. Although between 1961–91 employment in the services sector in Glasgow rose from 48 per cent of the workforce to 77 per cent, this was almost entirely the result of the loss of jobs in all the other major sectors. Employment in the primary, manufacturing and construction sectors fell by 17.3 per cent, 44.3 per cent and 15.2 per cent, respectively, between 1981–91, while service sector jobs rose by only 1.1 per cent – a net loss of over 41,000 jobs, much of it again to areas surrounding the city (Pacione 1995: 146). In recent years there has been considerable investment in the retail capacity of the city centre, which is now a major shopping centre, and in developing call-centres, but this again has not provided jobs relevant to the main groups in need – the long-term male unemployed living in the peripheral housing estates or in the inner-city. Investment in the retail capacity of the town centre and attempts to stimulate small and medium private sector enterprises have not made up for the loss of skilled, predominantly male, manufacturing jobs. As a consequence, Glasgow still suffers acutely from the 'jobs gap' that has been identified in many of Britain's inner cities (Turok and Edge 1999). Similarly in Middlesbrough attempts to replace this dramatic loss of employment and income through attracting inward investment in manufacturing and private sector services, most notably by the Teesside Development Corporation, comprehensively failed (Beynon *et al.* 1994).

In short, in both places there has been little growth in employment and such growth as has occurred has been in sectors that lack the potential to resolve the persistent unemployment problems that blight the local economy. As net VAT registrations – which indicate where entrepreneurial activity is developing in the local economy – demonstrate, in neither place is investment flowing into private sector activities that generate significant employment growth (Figure 4.1).

In the case of Glasgow the overall trend is sharply down, with the only signs of growth in real estate and in the public sector. In Middlesbrough, after a sharp fall in activity to 1995, there has been very little new activity in any major sector of the economy. This suggests that, while the condition of the local economy may not be deteriorating, neither is it improving from its very low level of activity. This is also borne out by the subdued rate of decline in unemployment in Middlesbrough. While Glasgow still has a large number of registered claimants, this figure has fallen considerably since 1996. In Middlesbrough, although the unemployment rate has fallen, the rate of fall is much less and bottoms out much sooner, indicative of a deeply depressed local economy.

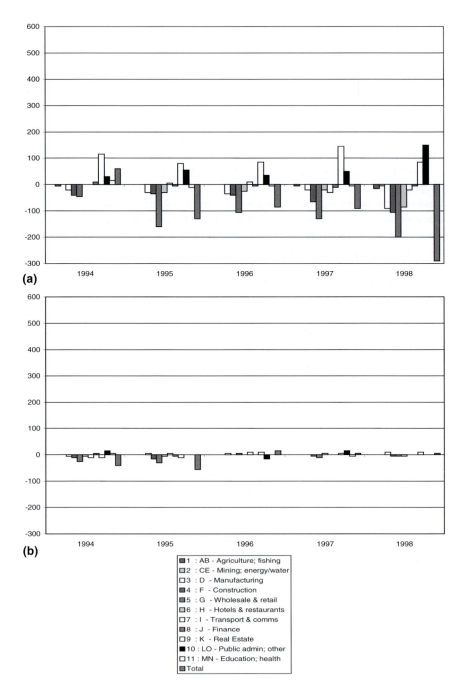

Figure 4.1 Net VAT registrations, (a) Glasgow and (b) Middlesbrough, 1994–8.[2]
Source: National Online Manpower Information Service (NOMIS).

The demise of the industrial bases of Glasgow and Middlesbrough has bequeathed problems of extreme deprivation and social exclusion. While in both places there have been some signs of recovery, and while there are pockets of relative wealth in particular wards and districts, the overall picture is one of pervasive need.

Of the ninety districts listed in the 1998 Revised Scottish Area Deprivation Index as the worst 10 per cent post-code districts (PCDs), fifty-seven were in Glasgow city. Of those outside of the city proper, a further twenty-two of these PCDs, particularly those in Paisley, Greenock North, and South Lanark, are on the boundaries of the city. Although Glasgow is by no means alone in suffering from high levels of poverty in Scotland, by all measures the extent and intensity of the problems faced by the city remain considerably higher than any other area. In the most recent analysis of the Intensity Measure of Deprivation, for example, Glasgow had the highest score of all Scottish Unitary Local Authorities, some 17 per cent higher than the next highest (Edinburgh) and considerably higher than the rest. This figure itself conceals the widely uneven distribution of poverty and social exclusion in the city (Figure 4.2), with particular concentrations in the northern and eastern areas around the city centre, and in the peripheral housing estates (Danson and Mooney 1998).

While not on the same scale as Glasgow and its hinterland, there are considerable problems of deprivation and poverty in Middlesbrough. Although there are

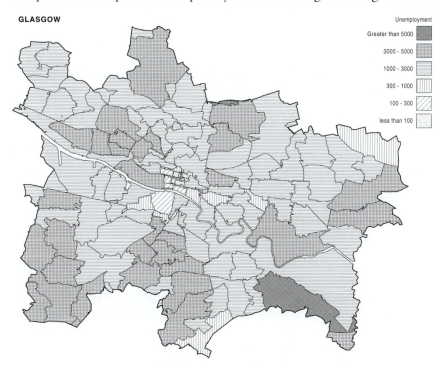

GLASGOW

Unemployment

Greater than 5000

3000 - 5000

1000 - 3000

300 - 1000

100 - 300

less than 100

Figure 4.2 Map of deprivation in Glasgow.[3]

some prosperous wards, the DETR's (2000) Index of Multiple Deprivation (IMD) reveals that the majority of wards in Middlesbrough rank highly in the index. Three – Pallister, Thorntree, and St Hilda's – are among the ten most deprived wards in England. Pallister and Thorntree form part of a large area of predominantly social housing, much of it of low quality and in a poor state of repair, which stretches across a large area to the south and east of the town centre. St Hilda's is a small area, again containing largely social housing, situated in what used to be both the original settlement and industrial iron-making core of Middlesbrough on the banks of the Tees just north of the town centre. Until 1998 St Hilda's was within the area controlled by the Teesside Development Corporation but has not noticeably benefited from any of the regeneration money that it administered. Housing in St Hilda's is in a particularly poor state of repair, much of it vandalised and empty, and beset by persistent rumours among local residents that the council is deliberately allowing it to deteriorate prior to demolition. There are no schools, shops or services within the area itself and the last remaining old people's home was closed by the council in 1999.

Low educational attainment is acute in these and other wards, as are problems of child poverty where four wards are among the worst ten nationally. Other notable problems include high and persistent unemployment and welfare dependency, poor health, and a lack of accessible health care facilities on many of the estates. These problems are compounded by the stigmatisation of the estate. For example, St Hilda is referred to as 'over the border' which, as Wood and Vamplew note, is used to imply on 'the wrong side of the tracks' or 'beyond the pale' (1999: 21). While St Hilda's is subject to a specific form of labelling, all of the estates in the town have a strongly insular character. This is in part a consequence of the dispersed nature of housing in the town, a deliberate policy imposed by the major industrial interests in the past spatially to fragment the working class and continued in the pattern of local authority housing (Beynon *et al.* 1994). The result is a series of dispersed communities with very little interaction with each other, with each fiercely defensive of its own turf.

This also in part contributes to the strong local intensity of deprivation in Middlesbrough. Local authority district comparisons produced as part of the IMD 2000 statistics demonstrate that, while Middlesbrough ranks very highly on many of the deprivation rankings, in the category of 'local concentration',[4] Middlesbrough ranks highest out of all 354 English local authority districts.

The existence of intense deprivation within the town's housing estates means that in addition to having very little local capacity, whether understood in terms of economic resources or social capital, these communities have few if any connections to those other parts of the local and regional economy that have been economically more successful. In the case of Glasgow, problems of isolation in the outer estates have likewise given rise to pockets of extreme deprivation. This is also the case, however, for those wards that directly adjoin the main retail centre of the city. The area immediately to the east of the city centre has been subject to repeated attempts at regeneration since the Glasgow Eastern Area Renewal (GEAR) project in the second half of the 1970s.[5] Nevertheless, it is still marked by

MIDDLESBROUGH

Rank of Index of Multiple Deprivation

Greater than 5000

3000 - 5000

1000 - 3000

300 - 1000

100 - 300

less than 100

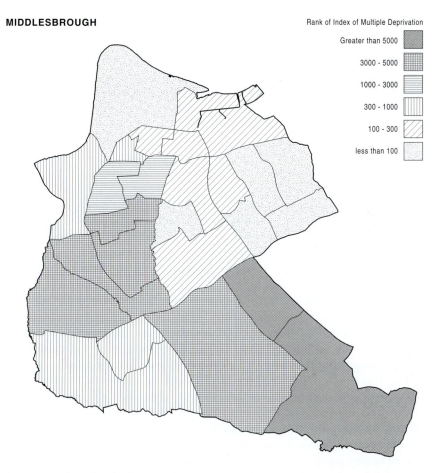

Figure 4.3 Index of Multiple Deprivation (IMD 2000) map of Middlesbrough.[3]

very low levels of economic activity and appears in stark contrast to the relative prosperity of neighbouring districts. The same is true to the south, where, facing the city centre across the Clyde, the Gorbals and Govan have remained largely untouched by new investment (Danson and Mooney 1998).

The locally-concentrated character of poverty in these places suggests that the model of the community-based social enterprise promoted by the current policy agenda should find there an environment rich in possibilities. The Third Sector might identify and exploit the latent capacities of such places by recycling whatever income and expenditure there is in the local economy to 'turn needs into markets' (Grimes 1997). There are clearly many unmet needs in both Glasgow and Middlesbrough. But, has the local civic and political capacity been there to respond? And if it has, in what ways has it responded to unmet need? How have the powers of place been mobilised to define and deal with local need?

Civic and political legacies

In both Glasgow and Middlesbrough the close relationships that existed in the past between a small set of dominant employers, trades unions, and local authorities, coupled with a general lack of social and cultural heterogeneity, has generated a corporatist and hierarchical political culture, resulting at times in considerable overlap between state and civic organisations. In both cities, the legacies of large mass-employing industries continue to affect the social and political landscape long after the industries themselves have shrunk or gone completely. In both Glasgow and Middlesbrough, social life was organised predominantly in relation to the workplace resulting in a particular gender division of labour – men in industrial workplaces, women in the home – and localised communities strongly identified with particular industries. However, similar industrial structures and divisions of labour were linked to strongly contrasting political cultures. In Glasgow, there was a very strong political culture mediated through highly-organised and militant trades unions, again emphasising the powerful links between spatially-defined communities and particular industries. Govan and the Gorbals, for instance, were strongly associated with the shipyards on 'Red Clydeside', an association that remains in spite of the fact that only a very small number of local people are still employed in what little remains of the industry. Participation in bitter industrial disputes, including such relatively recent events as the occupation of the shipyards in 1972 (Thompson and Hart 1972) and the extended fight to prevent the closure of the Ravenscraig steel plant in the early 1980s, strengthened the sense of community in many inner-city areas (Pacione 1995). This situation, however, produced a double dependency within working class communities on employers for jobs and wages and on trades unions for welfare and support. The demise of the main industrial base also meant the erosion of union power and wealth, leaving many inner-city communities isolated and very heavily dependent on state welfare at a time of sharp reductions in the level of welfare provision.

Further isolation and dependence was created as a consequence of the policy of rehousing inner-city communities in large peripheral housing estates and New Towns such as Cumbernauld, East Kilbride, and Livingstone during the 1960s and 1970s. A very high proportion of the new homes built in these areas, as well as in parts of the city centre, was in the form of high-rise flats which were relatively cheap to build and able to house large numbers at high densities. The problems associated with high-rise buildings are well-documented throughout Britain and Glasgow itself began to revise its high-rise strategy in the early 1970s. However, by that point the problems for the communities transferred to such housing in the peripheral estates and New Towns were already well established. Familiar problems of poor transport links, high unemployment, social and economic isolation, crime, substance abuse and ill-health quickly became endemic. A particular problem concerned access to shops and services since it was not until 1971 that any attempt was made to incorporate private sector development into the peripheral housing schemes (Pacione 1995: 163).

In Middlesbrough as in Teesside more generally, political culture developed in quite a different way to that of Glasgow. The current social geography of Middlesbrough is in large part a product of the pervasive and paternalistic influence of the main firms that controlled the town's industrial economy during the periods of very rapid growth in the nineteenth and early twentieth centuries (Beynon *et al.* 1994). Whereas in Glasgow the tradition was for social and welfare services to be organised through the trades unions and the local authorities, on Teesside such activities tended to be organised by the firms themselves, which built company towns around their main plants, while strongly influencing the character of trade unionism and union policies. With the establishment of the welfare state many of these services were supplied by local authorities but planning and investment decisions remained dominated by the interests of the large firms, refracted through a conservative local Labourism that was acutely tuned to the interests of 'local industry'. This produced a different form of dependency among local people to that in Glasgow, as the major industrial concerns manipulated the development of the town to prevent the growth of a militant organised labour movement that would challenge their interests. As Beynon *et al.* note,

> Through a selective provision of housing, roads, schools and other amenities, the steel and chemical companies developed an environment and social climate ideally suited to the reproduction of acquiescent and tractable labour forces. There was, quite deliberately, little opportunity created for waged employment other than in chemicals, steel and related industries. Partly because of this, the companies which led the development of the area exerted a particularly pervasive influence which extended beyond the relations of the workplace far into those of civil society.
>
> (1994: 53)

The result, which can still be seen in the distribution of social housing in Middlesbrough, is a series of estates, often adjoining, but housing very insular communities with little or no recognition of common interests or identities.

The dominant industrial cultures of Teesside and Clydeside, which did so much to shape the local society, have also established enduring political cultures. Although the local politics of both places have for some time been dominated by ingrained Labour Party establishments, this masks significant differences between them. While Labour politics on Clydeside was strongly to the left and prepared to be confrontational in its dealings with the major local employers, on Teesside the political establishment was much more dependent on and supportive of the major firms. The relative lack of autonomous worker organisation on Teesside – which had been actively prevented by employers via their encouragement of paternalistic company unionism – and, at least until the 1970s, apparent security of relatively well-paid local jobs, meant that the interests of capital coincided with those of the local Labour establishment, whose main interest lay in ensuring continuity. While both places, therefore, were characterised by very strong municipal political organisations, which in both cases were highly interventionist, their character was

very different. In the case of Glasgow, this was manifest in large-scale infrastructural planning schemes and centrally-organised social welfare programmes.
In Middlesbrough this took the form of business-oriented investment strategies
which assumed that the interests of local people would coincide with those of
private sector employers.

The enduring corporatist political cultures of both cities have had a significant
influence on the form and dynamics of the social economy. As we shall see in the
rest of the chapter, first, it has not lent itself to sustained advocacy and action from
below, and second, as a result of the gradual institutional hollowing out associated
with deindustrialisation, this has left the local state in an influential position. The
result in both places, albeit through very different routes and in respect of very
different manifestations of the social economy, has been to increase the central
control of regeneration activity, in both the mainstream and social economies, by
the local state. This is counter-intuitive in the context of the prevailing discourses
of devolved localism outlined in Chapters 1 and 2 that surrounds current advocacy
of the social economy for poor places. The logic of current expectations of the
Third Sector is that places with very severe problems of social exclusion – and
Glasgow and Middlesbrough are both firmly in that category – should be developing localised organisations, mobilising local capacities and local people. That it
seems in fact to be the local state that is playing the leading role, in many ways
serving to displace community-based activities or to fill the vacuums that their
absence causes, suggests that the current policy agenda is unwarrantedly optimistic. Significantly for the current study, it emphasises the lack of account being
taken in current social economy debates of the importance of place – local geographies and local histories – in the determination of social economy outcomes.

The social economy

Despite the similar problems facing Glasgow and Middlesbrough, the nature of
the social economy in each place is markedly different. Glasgow has come to be
closely associated with innovative and successful Third Sector activities, with the
social economy dominated by large-scale, highly-professionalised organisations.
These either deliver a wide range of services to people in one small area or provide
one type of service on a city-wide and even region-wide scale, in ways which echo
the statist provision of services. The social economy is highly centralised through a
series of intermediary and networking organisations that draw together key
members of local political élites, intellectuals and social economy animateurs. The
social economy in Glasgow is strongly supported by the state and has close links to
local political and administrative bodies, particularly to the city council through
Scottish Enterprise Glasgow (SEG),[6] national and European authorities (through,
for example, the Strathclyde European Partnership and the Scottish Executive)
and to higher education institutions located in the city (most notably the
Territorial Employment Research Unit (TERU) at Glasgow University).
There is, by contrast, comparatively little in the way of independent, small-scale
community-owned Third Sector activity.

Middlesbrough, in contrast, has a much weaker social economy. There are a few (five currently) local community-based social enterprises based in the town and adjacent housing estates, all of which lead a very precarious existence, and two larger and more secure organisations operating on a wider geographical scale to deliver services to particular sections of the Teesside population. Whereas the social economy in Glasgow is both a significant employer and service provider, in Middlesbrough the social economy is a fragmented and marginal activity relative to the welfare activities of local government and the national state, either tightly controlled and closely scrutinised or directly organised by the local state.

Glasgow

Although Glasgow perhaps more than any other part of the UK has come to be associated with the Third Sector development, to some extent that reputation is based on activities that have largely disappeared. Following the failure of many social enterprises during the early 1990s, changes in the priorities of regeneration policy and funding and the reorganisation of local government, the conditions that had made Glasgow a testing ground for innovative community-based activities largely evaporated. As a consequence many activities that are elsewhere in the UK increasingly carried out by the Third Sector largely independently of local government, in Glasgow now come under the auspices of a range of intermediary organisations controlled to a greater or lesser degree by the City Council. The corporatist legacy of an earlier of state provision thus lives on. This is not to say that there are no independent Third Sector organisations in the city – far from it. But they are in a minority. Only 17 per cent of those organisations identified as part of the social economy of the whole of Lowland Scotland were in fact social enterprises pursuing the goal of combining innovative and independent economic activity with community empowerment and local regeneration (McGregor *et al*. 1997: ii). However, those organisations that have been able to develop and grow wholly or largely independently of the local authority typically have been able to do so because they operate at a sufficiently large scale to insulate them from the many changes that have taken place affecting regeneration strategies in the area.

Glasgow's enduring reputation as a centre of social economy innovation stems in large part from the role played by the city throughout the 1980s as the centre of the largest social enterprise development programme in UK – the Community Business (CB) scheme. The CB programme began in the late 1970s in Paisley and was quickly extended to other parts of the city and to Strathclyde Region as a whole. From the early 1980s, the CB development programme was funded through the Urban Programme (UP) – regeneration funds provided by the UK government that were administered by the Scottish Office. In an arrangement that was unique in the UK, responsibility for the distribution of UP funds to community businesses was vested in an organisation established with the sole aim of promoting the community business model, Strathclyde Community Business, rather than local government or the Scottish Office.

Plate 4.1 Glasgow, Gorbals, 1960s tower blocks and current redevelopment.

Plate 4.2 Glasgow, Gorbals.

   Community businesses were given up to seven year's funding after which time they were expected to have become financially-independent and community-owned businesses. Although this scheme extended to cover most of Scotland, by far the greatest level of activity was in Glasgow. Several hundred community business were established there between the late 1970s and the early 1990s when the scheme was wound up. Although the theoretical model of the community business remains highly influential throughout the rest of the UK, particularly through the work of John Pearce who launched and ran the CB programme (Pearce 1993), only a small handful of the Scottish community businesses have survived (Hayton 2000). There are several reasons for the disappearance of the community businesses in Glasgow. First, funding criteria for the urban pro-gramme moved towards more holistic, area-based programmes such as the current Social Inclusion Partnerships and the Priority Partnership Areas that preceded them. At the same time, Local Enterprise Companies (LECs) took over responsibility for business development and saw their role as one of encouraging private sector development rather than regeneration (Hayton *et al.* 1993). Second, and more importantly, community businesses failed to fulfil the expectations of their funders. One of Glasgow's highest profile community businesses, Barrow-field, went into liquidation in 1989 despite being widely hailed as a replicable example of best practice (Hayton 2000: 196). As Hayton notes, by the early 1990s the CB scheme was really only able to be considered a success 'if success were to be measured by the amount of money that was being allocated to it and its inclusion in many regeneration strategies' (2000: 196). A growing body of academic analysis and policy reappraisal from the late 1980s onwards was increasingly finding that many of the projects operating were unsustainable in financial terms, were not cost effective, displacing rather than creating employ-ment and, in many instances, were not really community businesses at all. A wide range of voluntary sector organisations counted themselves into the community business scheme because, 'many initiatives realised that by using the "community business" label, they could gain access to resources that would not otherwise be available' (Hayton 2000: 197). As a consequence:

> The main outcomes were that many initiatives that were not community businesses were supported and there was a high failure rate as the emphasis was upon new starts rather than providing development support . . . [. . .] Funding had . . . been provided at a far higher level than the support framework was capable of absorbing effectively. The consequence was a failure to deliver. Community business obtained short-term benefits by over-selling but these were at the expense of the concept's longer-term credibility.
>
> (ibid.)

   Furthermore, other changes were taking place with significant ramifications for the social economy. In Glasgow, the reorganisation of local government in the mid 1990s, from two-tier (regional and town/city councils) to single-tier unitary authorities, has had important consequences for the social economy. In Glasgow the fiscal pressures unleashed by this process on the inner-city were of such magnitude that activities seen by many in the City Council as essentially marginal were cut back. The Chief Executive of the East End Partnership in Glasgow, for example, described how, following the break up of Strathclyde Region, the municipalist attitudes of the City Council came to prevail, generally favouring large-scale housing-led approaches to regeneration rather than smaller community-based activities. As a consequence of this, he concluded,

> I would say that across Glasgow there has been a sort of death of community organisations. . . . People simply got pissed off, fed up and walked away from it. And that on top of funding cuts, local authority budget cuts. Smaller councils mean smaller budgets and the non-statutory things go first. So there's been cuts in all of these budgets and community organisations that used to receive funding no longer do, so they've just naturally died over the recent years.

This perception is supported by evidence of a 'fiscal crisis' in Glasgow in the years immediately following the creation of the unitary authorities. The effect of separating the centre of Glasgow from its more prosperous suburbs, combined with a significant overall fall in population, was particularly harsh:

> Overall the gap between the inherited budgets from its [Glasgow City Council's] predecessors and its new spending assessments was 10.9 per cent, compared with a Scottish average of 1.5 per cent. Glasgow faced *severe* reductions in spending, and transitional arrangements were made to spread these over three years. In addition, the government built into the grant settlement assumptions that reorganisation would lead to efficiency savings in the bureaucracy. The cost to Glasgow was £7 million.
>
> (Carmichael and Midwinter 1999: 92)

In order to accommodate this significant drop in revenues, Glasgow City Council was required to introduce a £68 million package of spending cuts, partly through reductions in administrative costs (mainly through redundancies), in services and in grants to individuals and organisations. Data for the City Council cited by Carmichael and Midwinter reveal that these cuts actually increased between 1996–7 and 1997–8 (Table 4.1).

Table 4.1 Balancing the budget in Glasgow (£m)

	1996–7	1997–8
Cutting administrative costs	21.3	27.6
Cutting service provision	19.5	25.3
Cutting grants to other bodies	2.2	2.6
Total	43.0	55.5

Source: Carmichael and Midwinter 1999: 95, citing City of Glasgow Finance Department.

Given the heavy reliance of social economy organisations on local authority support, all three areas of spending reduction had a significant effect. Local government reorganisation served to undermine many of the few social enterprises that had managed to survive the reform of the Urban Programme and, more generally, greatly reduced the amount of local and community-based activity in the Third and voluntary sectors. This, combined with an overall reduction in the regeneration funds available through the Social Inclusion Partnership Fund and the increasingly competitive nature of the funding regime, eliminated many of the smaller and more precarious organisations from the Glasgow social economy. Such organisations have been unable to benefit either from a high degree of financial independence or from the protection of the public sector.

A major consequence of the collapse and discrediting of the community business model, and the subsequent shift of much more restricted funding away from small-scale community projects, has been to leave the current Glasgow social economy dominated by much larger scale organisations, many of them more closely integrated with the public sector than might otherwise have been the case. These take the form of a range of intermediary bodies whose task in Glasgow is, variously, to develop small private sector businesses, deliver and/or arrange training, and provide workspace for business start-ups. There are seven Local Development Companies (LDCs), established from the late 1980s to the early 1990s by the Glasgow Development Agency (now Scottish Enterprise Glasgow – SEG), which are situated in the main areas of deprivation in the inner city and in the peripheral housing estates.[7] In addition to these, and to some degree overlapping with them, are a range of Social Inclusion Partnerships (SIPs) established after 1997 with the reform of the Urban Programme. The SIPs are small area-based regeneration partnerships, similar to the *New Deal for Communities* projects in England, which have been awarded up to ten years funding to meet a range of targets, including the development of sustainable social enterprises (Sewell 1998). The SIPs themselves come under the auspices and oversight of the Glasgow Alliance which has a city-wide remit to co-ordinate development activity with LDCs, independent welfare organisations, health and education authorities, and LECs.

Responsibility for the development of social enterprises, which remains an explicit aim of at least some regeneration activity in the area despite the collapse of the CB programme, falls under the remit of all of these various organisations. Although many of these bodies are routinely described as constituting part of the social economy, they are in practice public sector quangos which deliver specific aspects of welfare provision, training and employment services and co-ordination at a local level on behalf of local and national authorities. As such they have tended to occupy spaces that might elsewhere be filled by more autonomous and independent Third Sector organisations providing an alternative to state provision rather than a conduit for it.

Glasgow, therefore, presents a paradox in terms of expectations and outcomes. Given Glasgow's enduring reputation as a hotbed of innovative Third Sector activity, and because of the sorts of assumptions about the equation of social exclusion and the social economy outlined in Chapters 2 and 3, we might reasonably expect a wide range of local and community-run social enterprises. In practice what we find is a much more ambiguous picture, one in which independent community-based activities, as the quote above suggests, have largely disappeared, to be replaced with a much more top-down and centrist form of regeneration activity. This is not to suggest that independent social enterprises have simply vanished from Glasgow, a few persist in spite of the many changes outlined above. Rather, it is to note that those social enterprises that have survived have done so because they are of a scale and type that has allowed them to ride out the changing fortunes and fashions of regeneration policy in the city. Importantly, they do not conform to the localised, community-owned vision of the social economy held by its current advocates elsewhere in the UK. Before considering these organisations that typify Glasgow's social economy, however, we will begin with one of very few organisations that in some respects comes close to the ideals of the social economy anticipated by policy-makers and outlined in Chapter 3, although in other ways it diverges significantly from them.

Most of those community businesses established in Glasgow in the 1980s were short-lived and almost all of those that had lasted through to the 1990s came to an end and went out of business following the retargeting of UP funds towards area-based schemes (Hayton 1993, 2000). One of the two survivors is Govan Workspace, formally established in 1981 though it originated in a Community Resource Centre formed in 1977.[8] It was therefore one of the first Community Businesses established in Scotland, predating the formation of Strathclyde Community Business itself. Following the collapse of Barrowfield, Govan Workspace is one of only very few social enterprises in Scotland that are still community owned and controlled wholly independently of any intermediary organisation or public sector body.

Since its formation, Govan Workspace has grown steadily, developing a succession of derelict industrial sites (a disused bakery site, an old school, and a former shipyard building) into managed workspaces for local firms. Although one-off grants were sought for some of these developments, from the outset Govan Workspace's main source of capital has come in the form of commercial loans and mortgages from private sector banks. The independence from the changing fashions among funding bodies that this has allowed is cited by the managing director as a significant factor in the project's survival and growth for over two decades. Another important factor has been the focused nature of the project's objectives. The purpose of the Workspace was, from the outset, not to attempt to provide the sort of wholesale local regeneration that many expect of the social economy, but – unusually for a social enterprise – to concentrate all its attention on the retention of private sector jobs and economic activity in one of the most deprived areas of the city. The Workspace sites now house over ninety firms employing over 500 people – 57 per cent of them living in Govan itself – engaged in a wide variety of mainly private sector activities. Until very recently, the project has not seen its role as one of delivering regeneration in any holistic sense because of a recognition from an early stage in the project's life that the problems of the area were simply too great for a small social enterprise to tackle. Instead, Govan Workspace has had a long-term development plan to create a secure, self-financing community-owned asset which can then become the springboard for other activities. By 2003 when the project anticipates that it will have paid off all of its outstanding mortgages and loans, it will be generating a substantial surplus which it will plough into new ventures, possibly further workspace development and youth training to attempt to tackle with some of the wider and very acute problems of the area.

Despite living up to many of the paradigms of social enterprise practice, Govan Workspace is currently atypical of the social economy in Glasgow and indeed sees itself as operating very much on the margins. Although its managing director is involved in the local Social Inclusion Partnership and has other connections to the many public and voluntary sector networks in Glasgow, he describes the Workspace as 'the leper colony' – operating largely in isolation from the highly-professionalised and centralised social economy of Glasgow as a whole. Part of this isolation he attributes to the fact that Govan Workspace is still known as a Community Business, which, because of the wholesale discrediting of the term, he believes puts his organisation at a disadvantage in a very competitive and fashion-conscious environment.

Elsewhere in Glasgow organisations that might once have been established as independent community businesses now tend to come under the auspices of much larger organisations. For example, Castlemilk Electronic Village, formed in 1998, has been set up as a subsidiary company of the Castlemilk Economic Development Agency (CEDA), one of the seven LDCs, and which itself forms part of a large, well-established local regeneration organisation, the Castlemilk Partnership.

The Electronic Village that CEDA has established is intended to be one of a new breed of social enterprises in Scotland that differ from the failed community business model in that they provide local services on the back of a non-profit company which trades in open markets in competition with private sector competitors. The project combines a small-scale intermediate labour market training programme – which takes up to fourteen local long-term unemployed people and trains them as internet designers and managers – with a multi-purpose internet service. The commercial firm is run by a combination of professional information technology (IT) staff and people employed from the training programme and offers a range of internet access and website hosting services to companies and other Third Sector organisations locally and across the city. As the project expands, it is hoped that in addition to the Intermediate Labour Market (ILM) scheme, the Electronic Village will be able to offer a range of free or subsidised internet services to the residents of the Castlemilk estate to overcome the problem of IT exclusion and the growing digital divide.

While the Castlemilk Electronic Village is being hailed as a success, which is important in a city which the idea of community business has been so thoroughly discredited, it is important to note that it could not have been launched without the backing of the larger organisation. Not only was the CEDA able to use its scale and established expertise to secure the capital funding required to launch the project, but it was also able to use its own computing needs to provide the Electronic Village with its first major 'customer'. However, the capacity of CEDA to do this is very unusual in Scotland. CEDA was one of the four original New Life for Urban Scotland projects launched by the Conservatives in 1987, and the only one in Glasgow. It is still receiving Social Inclusion Partnership Fund grants although not formally constituted as a SIP. As a result, the Castlemilk Partnerships have had a remarkably consistent and secure stream of public sector money for over fourteen years, especially when compared to many other projects and parts of the city. The result is a robust and multi-faceted organisation with a highly-trained and professional management team that has made very significant improvements in an area that was once a byword for urban blight. However, the implications of this in terms of the development of local social enterprises in Glasgow are ambiguous. Most importantly in the context of the localist agenda of much of the mainstream social economy debate, it belies the belief that successful social enterprises can somehow be wrought out of the latent capacities of poor people in poor places. Although Govan Workspace has, almost uniquely, been able to achieve something of the sort on behalf of the community it serves, revealingly its managing director is emphatic that he would not be able to repeat this under current conditions within Glasgow.

In contrast to the isolated development of the Workspace, the Electronic Village has been successful in large part because it has been able to draw on the economic and management resources of a much larger organisation. Furthermore, this organisation itself is funded largely through the public sector. This has enabled it to conduct careful market research and will enable it effectively to underwrite the Electronic Village until such time as it proves sufficiently competitive to stand alone. The degree of funding and other resources that have flowed into Castlemilk since the late 1980s, however, have not been available in most other parts of the city or, indeed, any other part of the UK.

In the East End of Glasgow, for example, another Local Development Company, the East End Partnership, the local SIP, and the Glasgow Alliance are also trying to develop new and existing social enterprises. There are some already in existence, most notably Calton Childcare which has been able to take advantage of renewed investment in child-care to create over sixty jobs for local women. This, however, is a rarity. Most of the other activities carried out under the umbrella of the East End Partnership are forms of training, job-search and small private sector business support that would previously have been delivered by a variety of smaller agencies. The amounts of funding available to the SIP with which to support social enterprises are very low indeed compared to the scale of local need. As one leading member of the local Glasgow Alliance Board, which oversees the distribution of funds in the area, remarked to us:

> [We have] a budget of £8.4 million over the next three years [for the East End], but we have only got a commitment for this year of £2.8 million and indicative figures for 2001–2, 2002–3. But the crux here is that existing

commitments have to be taken into consideration. So it's not new money. For example, last year [1998], to come within budget we had to close . . . five projects that comparatively speaking were fairly well known projects for issues in the area – good community-based projects like a neighbourhood hall, an adventure play park, a women's safety project, a print and communications unit. . . . But the [funding priorities] were budget driven, they weren't service delivery driven. So this year again because of the standstill budget, which means you cannot have inflation built into it, we are aware that in order to come within budget we are going to have to look very, very closely at twenty-seven projects.

As this implies, the situation in many parts of Glasgow is markedly different to that in Castlemilk. None of the twenty-seven projects mentioned in the quote above was ultimately shut down, but only because, according to another member of the local Board, the City Council was sensitive to the political implications of allowing them to close and then stepped in to prevent closure. More generally, however, elsewhere in Glasgow the lack of institutional and economic resources effectively means that local community projects, including social enterprises, are being closed down rather than being reestablished. Aside from new social enterprises in the process of being established under the auspices of larger organisations, there are currently very few organisations in the Glasgow social economy that are able to operate independently of the local authority, the SIPs or the LDCs.

Those that have been able to develop outside of this network include Glasgow's best-known and longest-established social enterprise, the Wise Group. The Wise Group has been able to weather the many changes to regeneration policy and funding in the city since its inception in the early 1980s, by virtue both of its scale of operation and the degree of influence it is able to wield at local, regional, and national levels. As suggested in the previous chapter, however, Wise is not a 'local' social enterprise in the sense that many proponents and practitioners of the social economy expect. It operates on many geographical scales and uses a professional staff to deliver a range of training services to large numbers of clients. In Glasgow alone Wise provides over 900 training places each year under its various ILM programmes. In addition to these, there are many more in subsidiary projects in other parts of Scotland and the rest of the UK (such as Newhamwise in London) and in indirectly affiliated organisations, such as those for which Wise provides consultancy services. The role played by Wise in the Glasgow social economy needs to be understood in two ways, first in terms of what it contributes to its clients via its own activities and second, the role it plays in influencing local and national social economy policy and practice.

In terms of its own activities, the Wise ILM model is well established and much emulated. Wise provides a year's on-the-job training for long-term unemployed people who, while they are within the scheme, produce socially useful goods and services for the people of Glasgow. Wise's core business centres on the use of its trainees to reclaim and landscape derelict open spaces and the 'back courts' of tenement blocks, to install insulation and security devices in social housing, and to restore forestry throughout west and central Scotland. While employed by the programme, trainees receive a weekly wage of around £120 per week, a programme of classroom-based as well as in-work training, and they are expected to treat the Wise job as though it was permanent. Since many of the tasks performed by Wise involve direct interaction with the general public, particularly where work is carried out in people's homes, the range of skills acquired by trainees is potentially very wide. The aim of Wise is to enable people who may have had little or no contact with the world of work to develop the full range of inter-personal and social skills which will help them move on into the open labour market at the end of their period of employment. More recently, Wise has broadened its client base to cover not just the long-term unemployed but also more 'job-ready' clients for whom it offers a more flexible and market-led course in the skills required by telephone call centres, a sector of significant employment growth. Wise has also launched a programme under which trainees help people with learning disabilities cope with the transition to paid work and independent living. The trainees under this scheme earn formal qualifications which allows them to move on into the care industry after they leave Wise.

In these various ways, Wise has been able to provide a very wide range of services for multiple communities throughout Glasgow and elsewhere and, as a consequence, has been widely held up as a model of Third Sector practice. That said, the image of Wise as an exemplary organisation is misplaced, and its experience is, in many crucial ways, atypical. This is most obvious in relation to its scale of operations. With a turnover of well over £20 million per annum and operations throughout the UK, Wise falls well outside the category of 'local' social enterprise. Then, nearly all of its income is derived from the public sector and, apart from some very shrewd and creative property deals that the organisation has been able to engineer, there is little prospect of its ever greatly reducing its dependence on public sector funding. Rather, Wise uses money that would normally be distributed as welfare payments directly to clients by the public sector to create local multipliers in the form of wages and social services. As such, Wise argues that it is using public money more productively than would otherwise be the case to justify the high cost of training its clients. As Wise points out, this money does contribute to providing people with new skills and constitutes a valuable contribution, in the form of wages and other expenditure, to the local economy.

The importance of Wise in the context of the Glasgow social economy, however, does not lie wholly in relation to its own particular practice. Wise also has been influential in the development of both local and, in the case of the New Deal 'Welfare-To-Work' scheme, national training and regeneration policies.[9] Wise has very close links with the Scottish Enterprise Glasgow, with other social enterprises, with policy-makers throughout the UK, and with other Third Sector intermediary agencies. Wise was, for example, instrumental in the creation by the Glasgow Development Agency of its own ILM scheme, the widely-praised Glasgow Works project. Glasgow Works creates temporary ILM programmes to provide targeted training in direct response to particular labour market demands (SEU 1998).

More recently established social enterprises in Glasgow have also been able to preserve their independence by operating on a large scale. One Plus, for example, is a child-care and support service targeted at lone parents living in the more deprived areas of the city. Although founded in 1980 as the Strathclyde Project for Single Parents, One Plus only began to operate as an independent social enterprise in 1987 after its grant was cut. Since then it has grown to offer a range of services, including advocacy and counselling services for young women and lone parents and has an annual turnover of over £3 million. Much of One Plus's recent growth has been enabled through a jointly-operated ILM project which it runs with Glasgow Works, funded through Scottish Enterprise Glasgow. The One Plus ILM offers training to young unemployed women, themselves often single mothers, which gives them both work-experience and an accredited qualification in child-care. Like many other child-care-based social enterprises in the UK, the aim of the One Plus training programme is that the women once trained will be able to establish their own small Third or private sector child-care companies, either independently or as franchisees of One Plus itself.

Although, unlike Wise, One Plus still operates through local (though not necessarily community-based) teams, the organisation none the less operates on a city-wide basis. Although very different in character from the Castlemilk Electronic Village, One Plus's recent growth has in part been enabled through a strategic partnership with Glasgow Works, which is operated almost wholly by Scottish Enterprise Glasgow and at considerable cost to the public purse. This is not intended in any way as a criticism of One Plus, but rather to highlight the point that what the social economy, in the context of Glasgow, is increasingly defined and constituted as a series of large-scale organisations which are linked in one of several ways to a highly integrated and centralised system of funding and control. Where an organisation, such as One Plus or Wise, is able to retain a great deal of independence over its operation (even if it is effectively subsidised by the local state to a very high degree) such a state of affairs can have very positive welfare benefits. In the case of One Plus this means the provision of services for lone parents that were not previously available through the statutory services. Wise's contribution is well-documented. However, as was illustrated in the case of the East End above, the constraints on funding, and the degree of political control of the regeneration agenda are not conducive to the development of small, independent social enterprises of the kind sought by current policy.

The example of Govan Workspace highlights some of the ambiguities and contradictions that exist within the social economy in Glasgow. As one of the first community businesses established under the Urban Programme, Govan Workspace can be seen as a successful example of just the kind of independent, self-financing, community-owned social enterprise currently expected by policy-makers. Although successful in achieving its stated aims, Govan Workspace does not in itself deliver much in the way of holistic regeneration for Govan. This is not intended as a criticism of the project, which measures its own considerable success in terms of the jobs it has created and maintained in Govan. However, it does illustrate that the expectations of the policy community – for jobs *and* welfare *and* empowerment – may well be beyond the capacity of small social enterprises working in areas of severe deprivation. In the case of Govan, the level of need has increased sharply during the lifetime of the Workspace as what little remained of the shipyards has been removed. The Workspace will certainly be able to increase its role in the future once it has paid off its mortgages (though, it should be noted, this will have taken over 20 years to achieve). Even so, the contribution that it will then be able to make will be limited compared to the scale of need in the local community. The sorts of ambiguities surrounding a project like Govan Workspace extend to cover much of Glasgow's social economy. The development of very large scale organisations such as Wise and One Plus, and the heavy involvement of Scottish Enterprise Glasgow in such projects as the Glasgow Works ILM scheme, has resulted in the conventional, small, community-based social enterprise becoming rare in Glasgow. While there is evidence, as in the case of the Castlemilk Electronic Village, that new forms of social enterprise are emerging, the dominance of the regeneration agenda by Glasgow City Council and the network of intermediary bodies and development companies, suggests that the bulk of the activities that might be expected to be carried out in a more autonomous and independent social economy will continue to be situated in organisations close to the public sector. The 'professionalisation' of the Scottish regeneration industry and the widespread demoralisation of deprived communities also suggests that the prospects for developing empowering community-owned projects are limited. This does not necessarily mean that the form of the social economy in Glasgow and the surrounding region will be less successful as a result (the 'community-owned' Community Business Programme was, after all, disastrous in economic terms). However, it does mean that the model of the social economy that is emerging is very different from the bottom-up, community-driven expectations of the academic and policy communities.

Middlesbrough

As noted earlier, the social economy in Middlesbrough is smaller, weaker and more marginal than its equivalent in Glasgow. Whereas Glasgow has at least some social economy presence in all parts of the city – albeit unevenly – in Middlesbrough the social economy is much more fragmented and sporadic, notable by its absence. This marked difference between Glasgow and Middlesbrough can to some extent be attributed to the different ways in which regeneration funds have been distributed in Scotland and England in recent decades. While in Scotland the Urban Programme was organised centrally by the Scottish Office and, for an extended period, aimed specifically at the development of social enterprises, this was not the case in England. Regeneration funds have tended to come under the control of local authorities and other local and regional agencies, most notably Training and Enterprise Councils (TECs) and Government Offices for the Regions, and the degree of emphasis on social economy development has as a consequence been very varied. Enthusiasm for and receptivity to the development of the social economy varies as a consequence of variation in local civic and political cultures. Active support for social enterprise development has only developed relatively recently in many places, greater attention having been paid to forms of regeneration based on investment by the private sector, either attracting large-scale investment projects and/or the in situ development of small and medium-sized enterprise clusters.

The nature of the current social economy in Middlesbrough provides one example of the effects of this sort of approach to regeneration in places in which community-based organisations have traditionally been seen as marginal to private sector-led economic development and public sector welfare provision. Middlesbrough has recently lost a number of organisations that have in the past potentially been key elements of the infrastructure of social economy development – most notably the local co-operative development agency. City Challenge funds won by the local authority were used to build a large Morrison's Supermarket (part of a large private sector retailing company operating throughout the north of England) in the East of the town rather than to invest in local capacity. Most recently (2000), the council has contracted out much of its direct service delivery to a new partnership organisation owned jointly by the council and a private sector firm. The new company, Middlesbrough Direct, which will effectively replace the council as a service provider throughout the town, includes no direct representation from the Third Sector and has only one voluntary sector representative on its board. In some other parts of the UK (Bristol, for example, discussed in Chapter 5) local councils have deliberately sought to devolve aspects of service provision to the Third Sector as a means of developing community-based economic development. In contrast, in Middlesbrough the existing social economy has been bypassed in favour of what is, in effect, service privatisation. This, combined with the highly bureaucratic way in which Middlesbrough administers project funds, has been seen by many people to signal a lack of belief in the social economy and community-based regeneration on the part of senior council staff and local councillors. Instead, they are seen to favour larger scale and more immediately cost effective (i.e. cheaper) private sector-led solutions.

As a recent Report from the Joseph Rowntree Foundation examining *Neighbourhood Images in Teesside* found, there remains a strong sense of and commitment to the local community on the part of residents even in Middlesbrough's most hard-pressed areas (Wood and Vamplew 1999).[10] Despite this, local people are currently unable to translate this sense of community into concrete social economy initiatives, largely because the resources and infrastructures to support such activities are absent or have been diverted to other uses. The nature of the problems faced by Middlesbrough, the nature and history of local people, and the attitude of the local authority have conspired to hinder the effectiveness of such social economy activities as do exist there.

The existing social economy on Teesside can be divided into two types of organisation. The more successful of these comprises a small number of organisations which operate throughout the area of the former Cleveland County, which was replaced with smaller unitary authorities, including Middlesbrough Town Council, in 1995. The second group consists of a small number of community-based social enterprises situated in various locations around the town. Despite the incidence of poverty and exclusion throughout Middles-brough, there are currently only five such organisations operating there. In all but one case, that of a newly established *New Deal for Communities* project (which, at the time of writing, had not established any concrete organisation on the ground), these projects have had a very limited impact and are leading a very precarious existence.

Of the first group of organisations, the most successful based in Middlesbrough itself is the Community Campus '87 project for young people with special housing needs and young women needing secure sheltered housing.[11] Community Campus '87 provides a mixture of housing, holistic social support and work training, by using the refurbishment of its properties to provide work experience for its tenants. The work of the tenants increases the housing stock owned by the project which, in turn, provides more training places to fund and refurbish more properties. Community Campus has been able to grow in this way because the very depressed condition of the local housing market allows it to buy empty and often derelict buildings very cheaply.

As its name suggests, Community Campus '87 was founded in the late 1980s by a group of local housing officers who were increasingly dissatisfied with the poor service being given by the statutory agencies to those clients in the greatest need. Increasing numbers of people with severe needs were being referred back to the officers concerned because they did not have the resources to manage properties once they had been allocated to them. Community Campus was established to provide a more supported route into independent living for the most vulnerable local people, incorporating housing, work place training, and long-term social support. The self-generating process of using work experience to develop skills in clients and create further housing units is one that has since been adopted in other parts of the UK (for example, Project John in Cumbria) where similar conditions prevail. In this way people in housing need can acquire properties cheaply or even freely in a severely depressed housing market.

However, the success of Community Campus has not been repeated in some of Middlesbrough's other social enterprises, most notably in those situated on local social housing estates. The St Hilda's Partnership, for example, originated in 1993 when a group of concerned local residents and the local authority joined forces to examine the needs of the community living in a relatively small housing estate in the former ironmasters district of the town. The Partnership was intended to bring together representatives of statutory agencies, the local authority, Teesside TEC, church organisations, private sector bodies, and Teesside University to tackle the wide range of social and economic problems in the area. It originally targeted five main areas: Employment and Training, Youth and Leisure, Community Crime Prevention, Housing and the Environment, and Heritage and Tourism. These various priorities were to have been delivered through the Partnership itself and a series of small and community-owned businesses. There were also ambitious plans that the project would develop Middlesbrough's famous transporter bridge as a tourist attraction to bring additional resources into the area.

Plate 4.3 St Hilda's, looking north towards Billingham.

Plate 4.4 St Hilda's.

In practice the co-ordinated actions have not transpired and there is a general feeling among project staff that they have been let down. Far from creating more local services in the area, the local authority has closed down the only remaining local school, further isolating an already stigmatised community. This added to a sense of alienation from and mistrust of the local authority. On the St Hilda's estate empty houses are not being allocated to new tenants, repairs to housing have been halted and other empty buildings, including several important examples of the town's heritage of industrial architecture, are being allowed to rot or be demolished by vandalism. Despite a strong residual sense of community among local residents, the population of the area is falling sharply (Wood and Vamplew 1999). To compound problems of despair and disinvestment, the Partnership itself has suffered severe setbacks. Local youths have vandalised the youth training unit so repeatedly that it has been closed down for long periods. Sections of the local community feel that they are not adequately represented by the project and have ceased participating in its activities. The proposed tourism centre based around the transporter bridge has come to fruition but without the direct involvement of the St Hilda's Partnership. Despite its involvement in planning the centre, the Partnership was left out of the implementation of the project. All of these problems have combined to make it very hard for the project to achieve its outputs and, therefore, for managers to secure the funding to continue. There are severe doubts that existing funding will be renewed after 2003 even if the Partnership remains solvent until that point in time.

Although in better shape than St Hilda's, the Grove Hill 2000 project is also precarious. Grove Hill 2000 was established in 1996 by a group of local residents concerned at the lack of provision of social and training facilities in the area. Despite having a very poor relationship with the local authority from the outset, Grove Hill was able to raise funds from the City Challenge scheme to construct a purpose-built community centre, comprising a café, a child-care unit, and a small business space in a large housing estate. Because of a pervasive mistrust of the local authority among local residents, Grove Hill had tried to ensure its independence by completing its own funding bids without the help of the council's economic regeneration team. Although these bids were successful, it has been impossible to develop the degree of independence to which the project aspired. The local authority remains the 'accountable body' for funds coming into the area from national or European sources, and as such maintains very tight control over the ways in which the project can spend its income. In practice this means that although technically owned and run by local residents, Grove Hill 2000 can have any of its management decisions vetoed by the local authority or delayed by the bureaucratic way in which regeneration funds are administered. In the name of accountability, therefore, the local authority restricts the access of the project to its own funds. As a consequence it has deprived the project of the degree of flexibility and cash-flow that a private sector company might take for granted. Despite the difficult relations with the local authority, Grove Hill has managed to open a child-care facility employing local women, a small video-editing and printing unit, and a café run by and for local people. The project's more ambitious plans to develop a local television studio and editing suite have, however, been halted by the council after second-hand cameras and equipment were bought for the sum of £65,000 by Grove Hill without approval and without going through the correct purchasing procedures. This resulted in the council imposing even tighter restrictions on the project, further increasing tensions with staff and residents.

Although Grove Hill continues to employ local residents to run all aspects of the project, and sees this as a virtue of the local social enterprise, elsewhere the lack of management skills among local people has almost proved disastrous. Although now the largest and possibly most secure of the community-based projects in Middlesbrough, the Langridge Initiative Centre (LIC) was nearly closed down by the local authority because of the managerial inexperience of residents. Serving the Berwick Hills and Park End estates to the south east of the town, LIC was launched in 1992 by local residents and the local authority in an attempt to tackle the very high and persistent levels of unemployment among young people on the estates. LIC was intended to provide both formal training towards recognised qualifications as well as to establish a small ILM scheme and a range of community businesses. It quickly became apparent, however, that the original staff, all of whom were local residents, lacked the necessary management skills and the project failed to achieve output targets, in terms of the number of training places taken up and the number of qualifications obtained, and was losing money. Despite a number of changes in senior staff by 1998 the problems had not been resolved and the Langridge Centre was given one year to deal satisfactorily with these issues or face closure by the local authority.

A new non-resident professional manager was subsequently appointed, and has been able to reverse the fortunes of the Centre. New courses have been introduced using professional training staff and the number of local people taking up training places has increased, as has the number leaving with qualifications. The Centre has been able to generate income through the establishment of a café for local people, renting out workspace to small businesses that it has helped establish, and the provision of child-care. Although the Centre manager acknowledges that LIC will never be grant free, the project is now able to generate enough income, much of it from the local authority in the form of service level contracts, to cover its running costs. New capital projects, however, still have to be funded through one-off grants from a range of funders including the EU, the National Lottery and Single Regeneration Budget (SRB) bids. The Centre has also recently been recognised as a Further Education college, giving it, as a result, access to more secure sources of funding. The residents of the estates served by the project are now finally seeing the development of a more viable (if not independent) social enterprise. The troubled history of LIC suggests, as was evident with many Scottish community businesses, that expecting the residents of impoverished communities spon-taneously to develop a range of skills and competencies in the running of social enterprises is unrealistic and can place severe burdens on those people as a result. It is, of course, difficult to see how local people are to acquire managerial skills other than via learning-by-doing and this inevitably has risks attached to it.

That said, the project still faces familiar problems concerned with the bureaucratic handling of funding. For particular projects or training courses, for example, the local authority will only provide up to 50 per cent of the dedicated funds in advance. The remainder is retained by the council and only becomes available to LIC once the 'need' for the course or project has been proven, a proof based wholly on quantitative outputs. This means that planning for growth and investment is made even more problematic since LIC cannot guarantee that it will even get the funds already set aside for it, let alone renew them in the future. It also raises the possibility that if the council unilaterally deems that need has not been proven, projects and courses in the early stages of their development will simply be scrapped with potentially negative consequences for both local residents and the credibility of the project.

In addition to the heavy bureaucratic burden and tight monitoring that Middlesbrough Council imposes on the few independent social enterprises in the town, it has also sought to spawn its own version of the social economy. In 1997 Middlesbrough Council established its own organisation managed by its regeneration team with the specific remit to establish community businesses. Combiz was intended to work:

> with the Private Sector to identify potential business ideas and Combiz will conduct market research and feasibility studies, and help with the production of business plans and cashflows to ensure that only ideas which have long-term viability are established.
>
> (Middlesbrough Council undated internal policy document)

This plan was developed in 1995 partly because resources available to the regeneration team were being reduced and it needed to find more cost-effective ways of using those that remained. Research by the Council brought them into contact with Tayside Community Business (TCB) in Scotland, which was at that time being heralded as a new model of social enterprise development (Hayton 2000). Once the core enterprises had been established by Combiz, ownership of the firms would pass to local people and employees assisted by both Combiz, acting as a form of public sector management consultant, and non-executive directors co-opted from participating private sector companies. To date, Combiz has established eight such 'community businesses' accounting for approximately thirty jobs held by previously long-term unemployed people. However, although these are claimed to be social enterprises, in practice they are conventional small private sector companies that had had little or no community involvement. Indeed, when asked how much community participation there had been in the establishment and running of these 'community' enterprises, one council officer happily stated, with a silent cheer, that there had been none – the implication being that involving local people would have been deeply problematic.[12] The companies in question produce a variety of goods and services and have not all survived. A company providing maintenance of vertical access platforms was sold by the Council to a private sector company. Nortech, which fitted and repaired garage doors, was unprofitable and closed down. Of the others, only Telebiz Training, which combines commercial IT and communications training for local firms with training for local unemployed residents, operates in a way that would be conventionally described as characteristic of the social economy.[13] Although the Council has recently renewed its commitment to developing and supporting Combiz, the original project was performing so poorly by 1998 that it was effectively frozen – with no new businesses being developed, no development activity, no dedicated funds and no full-time member of council staff. Following the appointment of a new chief executive in 1997, the council halved the number of regeneration staff working in the economic development department. This adversely affected both Combiz and the town's other social enterprises which had often relied on particular council officers to mediate relations with the local authority.

There are some signs of renewed interest in the social economy on the part of Middlesbrough Council, partly in response to changes in national policy following the Local Government White Paper and the publication of the Social Exclusion Unit's latest strategy document (SEU 2000). Even so, provision on the ground in Teesside remains fragmented and vulnerable. Those few social enterprises that have been able to survive are attempting to develop joint capacity in the form of regular networking meetings among themselves, but this is very recent and has yet to result in the formation of any formal social economy co-ordinating organisation. The few successful organisations, such as Community Campus, provide a specialist set of targeted services for particular client groups and, while they may assist other, area-based, projects, they do not offer much in the way of general regeneration. Where that might be expected to take place, in the small, nominally independent, community-based organisations, the limited capacity of local residents to manage complex social enterprises and the often obstructive attitude of the local authority combine to prevent anything substantial taking root. Given the scale of need in Middlesbrough and the concentration of deprivation and other social ills in very small areas, as in the case of Govan Workspace, this would be, perhaps, too much to expect. As the case of Glasgow illustrates, the development of successful social enterprises entails the conversion of needs into markets, and as such there has to be some minimal market capacity to enable that to take place. Even in a mainstream economy as large and diverse as that of Glasgow, such capacity is limited. In Middlesbrough, the resources available to create such a market barely exist within the stagnating local economy, or within a population that has been accustomed to top-down provision either from the major employers, from the local authority, or from both. This has left the local authority itself as the only viable source of funds for and, to a significant degree, animateur of the social economy, and again, as we have seen, its role in these regards has been problematic in many ways. This raises serious questions about the capacity of the social economy in such places to conform to the policy expectation that it can play a major role in regeneration. Furthermore, although the nature of the socio-economic problems faced in Glasgow and Middlesbrough is similar, the civic and political cultures of the two places are significantly different and this has consequences both for the expectations placed on the local social economy and for its capacity to meet those expectations.

Conclusion: the powers of place and scale

Both Glasgow and Middlesbrough suffer from problems caused by the collapse and/or withdrawal of long-standing and ingrained industrial cultures. This has left large groups cut off both from traditional sources of employment but also, and perhaps more importantly in the longer term, from those institutions that most served to shape community identity. In both places the role of the local state – by default or design – has become important, though the outcome has been different. In the case of Glasgow, earlier experiments with a strongly localised and independent form of social enterprise – the community business – came to a halt because of failure and the changing fashions of regeneration thinking and funding. It has been replaced by a highly organised, city-wide and area-based network of semi public sector organisations. This form of professionalised and carefully controlled social economy differs sharply from the sort of community-based and animated vision that most contemporary theorists and politicians have in mind and which, ironically, is most commonly attributed to Glasgow itself.

In Middlesbrough the local state itself has occupied the social and economic space that elsewhere might be used by local people to develop a more autonomous social economy. But this has not meant sustained or serious commitment. By using regeneration funds to establish the council-run Combiz over more independent organisations, by imposing onerous accountability structures and by diverting council spending to the private sector rather than the Third Sector, the local authority in Middlesbrough has shown lacklustre commitment to the social economy. Importantly, however, there is still some evidence of 'social entre-preneurship' among local people, albeit infrequently and typically on a small scale. In Middlesbrough, which has not been overwhelmed by the slick professionalism of much that takes place in Glasgow, those setting up and running social enter-prises are often local residents – Grove Hill 2000 and the St Hilda's Partnership are both examples of this. Even in circumstances in which those running the projects are not local to the area, as in the case of the Langridge Centre, there is a high degree of commitment to developing local capacity for local communities (Wood and Vamplew 1999). However, the enthusiasm of social economy activists is being placed under considerable strain by the interventionist attitudes of the local authority and, as in Glasgow, also by changes in socio-economic structure that are creating a declining generation of community activists.

The very different structure of the social economy in these two former indust-rial areas suggest that, even for places where the patterns and causes of social need are apparently similar, local institutional and civic cultures are very important in shaping outcomes. That said, the relationship between the social economy and place is very ambiguous in both. On the one hand, the local context of the particular urban area, its particular industrial, political, and social history and the spatial legacy of that, has clearly influenced the structure of social economy provision. In the case of Middlesbrough, the fragmented nature of local communities and the top-down approach to regeneration adopted by the town council means that whatever limited capacities might exist at grass-roots level, there is little opportunity for them to develop. In the case of Glasgow, the corporatist style of the city council (in contrast to the more dispersed and experimental approach of the Strathclyde Regional Council), combined both with a constraint of available resources and a recent history of community business failure, has produced a tightly controlled and prescribed form of social economy which operates at only a very small remove from the public sector. In both cases, the nature and structure of the local social economy has in large part been a product of the specificities of place. As we saw in the case of the East End of Glasgow where ostensibly local decision making was, in practice, centralised, and in Middlesbrough where the local authority has effectively tried to run the social economy from its own offices, the *scale* at which control is exercised also matters. The point is not that the local state has in some sense misappropriated the idea of the 'local' social economy because, as was seen, particularly in the case of Glasgow, independent social economy organisations themselves may have to operate on a large scale to compete and survive, a tendency reinforced by the failure to establish very localised social enterprises in the 1980s. Rather, our argument is that the scales at which Third Sector interventions are appropriate, as well as the nature of the way in which they operate and their relationship to the local state, will necessarily vary between places. While the corporatist nature of the social economies in both Glasgow and Middlesbrough undoubtedly leads to problems, it is important to understand why the Third Sector should come to operate at a city- or even region-wide scale rather than that of the local community. Why, in other words, should social economy practices so clearly rooted in place be apparently so blind to the specificities of the communities they are supposed to serve?

One answer to this may be that social enterprise solutions as prescribed by the localist agenda outlined above are simply not possible or relevant in some places. Ironically given the UK government's insistence on the greater use of self-help regeneration strategies for the very poorest communities, including the greater development of social economy organisations, it may be advocating a solution that relies on the existence of those features of local political, economic, and social life that the so-called 'worst estates' and most excluded people and places most significantly lack. But there is more. In places in which the institutions of civil society are poorly developed, all too often the local state, in pursuit of accountability and accepted notions of value for money or because of ingrained bureaucratic practices, has tended to close down the spaces within which the social economy might develop as an independent and community-controlled alternative. In Glasgow, despite its reputation for Third Sector innovation, the consequence of recent changes in the structure of the local state, the move away from the community business model and the controlling influence of the city council, has effectively removed the space opened up by the development of the community business model. In Middlesbrough the traditional political culture of the town council – based on top-down service delivery to deferential voters – never allowed such space in the past and there is little evidence of any likely change in the immediate future.

Our aim is not to suggest that the local state is necessarily inimical to the development of successful social enterprises. Some of the more successful and innovative projects cited above and in the previous chapter are heavily dependent upon support from the local or even national authorities. Most are still, after all, funded by and through them. The point we wish to make, instead, is that the practices of the local state are the product of local institutional checks and balances. In the context of severe deprivation, weak opposition, and insufficient institutionalisation of civic activity, the result has been a centralised, bureaucratic approach, often plagued by an audit culture, never quite convinced by the powers of bottom-up mobilisation of the social economy.

5 The distributed social economy
Bristol and Tower Hamlets

Introduction

The experience of the social economy in Bristol and Tower Hamlets has been quite different from that in Glasgow and Middlesbrough. It is less state dependent, more organisationally distributed, and able to draw on a wider base of opportunity. Although these two urban areas are very different in terms of their size and structure – the former is a large, prosperous city in its own right while the latter is only one part of a much larger metropolitan area, a global city – there are important similarities between them. Both contain very varied populations, some elements of which, particularly ethnic minority communities, have suffered disproportionately from problems of poverty and social exclusion. Although both places, like Glasgow and Middlesbrough, have experienced the contraction of mass-employment industries and the cultural and social systems that developed around them, these have been more extensively replaced by new industries and/or new social structures which have had important transformative effects.

As a consequence, both places have a much more varied and fluid civil society, comprising a mixture of different cultures, languages and traditions, different and changing economic classes, and old and new communities. This, we will argue, has had an important impact on defining needs as well as capabilities in the social economy. A further similarity between Bristol and Tower Hamlets is the close proximity of small areas of severe deprivation to larger areas of extreme wealth, in contrast to Glasgow and Middlesbrough where small areas of affluence are adjacent to much larger areas of poverty. Bristol is prosperous, with poverty clustered in small pockets of the inner-city and some peripheral housing estates. Tower Hamlets is a borough marked by extremes of poverty and exclusion (albeit in different ways in different communities), but increasingly integrated into the buoyant economy of London. We argue that this adjacency has helped to cushion and nurture the social economy. A final similarity between the two urban areas is the historically secondary role of local state involvement in the development of Third Sector activities, in sharp contrast to Glasgow and Middlesbrough. This has influenced the types of Third Sector activity that have evolved and the balance of responsibility between different types of agency in the social economy.

This chapter, therefore, continues our exploration of the powers of context, by examining the effect of social and cultural heterogeneity, institutional pluralism, and mainstream economic vitality, on the form and potential of the social economy. Both places are host to a range of social enterprises that have developed and survived for a variety of reasons of which the role of local state is just one. Bristol, for example, has a long history of non-mainstream movements with strong roots in community and social development. Similarly it has a long-established environmental movement which has spawned some of the more enduring and successful social enterprises in the city. In Tower Hamlets, although there is a long history of voluntary sector activity within the borough, reflecting the persistence of poverty in the area, the nature and context of civil society is very different. Not only is Tower Hamlets home to a wide variety of ethnic communities and different class identities, but it is also part of the wider society of London as a whole. This offers organisations operating within the borough the opportunity to draw on the resources of social and political networks from many different spatial scales that are not available to smaller, more isolated or less varied places.

We begin the chapter with an account of the local context in which social economy projects have developed in Bristol and Tower Hamlets. This includes the nature of the local economy, the geography of social deprivation, the nature of civil society, and the specific political culture in each place. While the context of place has helped shape the social economy, so too, reciprocally, has the character of the social economy influenced the nature of place. The second part of the chapter examines the nature of the local social economy in each to illustrate the ways in which these various factors have contributed to or hindered its development. The chapter concludes with an appraisal of how the social economies of Bristol and Tower Hamlets differ from each other and from those in Glasgow and Middlesbrough.

The economic context

Whereas the current problems of Middlesbrough and Glasgow can in large part be attributed to the demise of old industrial economies, the economic evolution of Bristol and Tower Hamlets has been rather different. Both have certainly seen the demise of older, mass-employment industries (the docks and associated industries in Tower Hamlets, tobacco, confectionery and engineering in Bristol) but these have been replaced by other growth industries and much greater rates of new firm formation, as indicated by net VAT registrations in the second half of the 1990s (Figure 5.1).

However, the fruits of economic success have not been distributed evenly throughout the resident population. Consequently, in both places, albeit in different ways and on a different scale, economic change has produced areas of poverty and social exclusion cheek-by-jowl with areas of considerable wealth.

In the case of Bristol, following from its early prosperity as a trading port, manufacturing industries grew up to process incoming commodities from the colonies. The chocolate and tobacco industries were the most prominent of these, supported by ancillary industries such as printing and packaging and light engineering. The engineering capacity of the city contributed to renewed growth

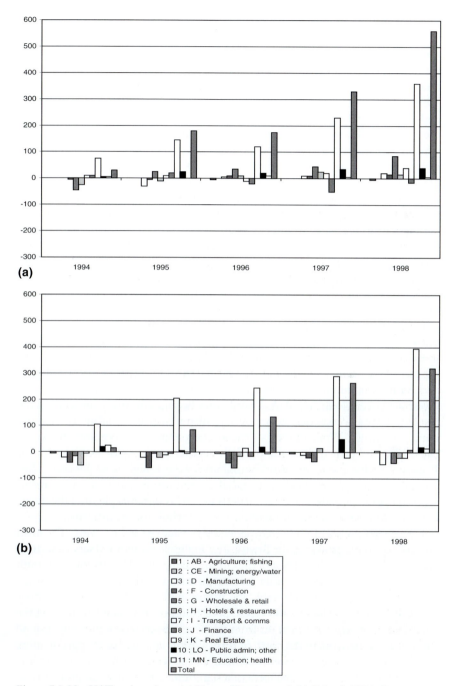

Figure 5.1 Net VAT registrations, (a) Tower Hamlets and (b) Bristol, 1994–8.

Source: National Online Manpower Information Service (NOMIS).

and change during the early twentieth century with the development of defence-related manufacturing, particularly of aircraft (Boddy *et al.* 1986). The strength of the city's industrial base and the growing significance of military production from the 1930s onwards meant that Bristol was to a large extent protected from the main periods of decline in UK manufacturing during the depression of the 1930s and, subsequently, during the recessions of the 1980s (Boddy *et al.* 1986; Bassett 1996: 532–3). As a centre of defence aviation technology and production Bristol and its hinterland benefited considerably from the high defence spending during the 1980s. As Bassett notes, while manufacturing industry and the economy in general were in sharp decline throughout the UK in the 1980s as a consequence of general recession, overall employment in Bristol continued to grow in both the manufacturing and services sectors (1996: 543). According to Boddy *et al.*, Bristol's rapid decline of older forms of manufacturing was offset by newer industries and the equally rapidly growing services sector (1986: 19). This long period of relatively stable prosperity in Bristol was broken only in the early 1990s with the scaling back of the military aerospace industry as part of the 'peace dividend' following the collapse of the Soviet Union. Between 1989–91 employment in the aerospace industry fell by 23 per cent accompanied by a growing realisation that Bristol no longer had the industrial diversity nor growth potential that had sustained it during earlier periods of crisis (Bassett 1996).

During the 1980s it became apparent that the general prosperity of Bristol was not shared equally or equitably among the population as a whole. Parts of the inner-city, particularly the areas around St Pauls, Easton, and Lawrence Hill to the east of the centre and which are the main centres for Bristol's Afro-Caribbean and Asian communities, had been deprived of both public and private sector investment over a long period. As a result, they became effectively cut off from the rest of the city as a consequence of poverty, unemployment, racial discrimination, crime, and drugs. While the rest of the local economy was booming during the late 1970s and early 1980s, the officially registered unemployment rates in St Pauls among the ethnic minority communities were as high as 42 per cent. This, accompanied by active and systemic racial discrimination and police harassment, sparked riots in St Pauls in the early 1980s which brought the plight of the inner-city communities to the attention of the city as a whole for the first time.

Uneven development was also experienced outside of the city centre. The main areas of economic growth in the Bristol area, in the electronics and service sectors, are located to the north and east of the city and along the M4 corridor. The south of the city, by contrast, steadily lost employment with the closure of some traditional industries, most notably the twenty-nine-acre Wills cigarette factory site in 1989 with the loss of 4000 jobs. Poor transport planning left much of the south of the city effectively cut off from the new industries concentrating around the motorway network to the north of Bristol. Although this has changed in more recent years, with even the south of Bristol experiencing effective full-employment, it has left its mark in the form of a significant legacy of social problems on the housing estates there. For example, on the Hartcliffe and Withywood Estate, although unemployment is low, the problems of low educational attainment, crime and, in particular, drug and substance abuse remain high.[1]

Similarly, in Tower Hamlets the highest levels of economic deprivation are still to be found in the borough's large ethnic minority populations and in areas of social housing formerly associated with the docks (Eade 1997; Foster 1999). None the less, the evolution of the local economy has been fundamentally different. This is partly because of its own particular industrial history associated with the London Docks and their demise during the 1970s and 1980s, but also because Tower Hamlets is a part of the wider London economy. With the increasing encroachment of the financial services industries of the City of London upon its western margins, Tower Hamlets has also become host to new elements of the global economy (Eade 1997). Historically, the main source of employment in the borough had been through the London Docks and associated industries such as warehousing, timber, potteries, and engineering (Foster 1999: 17). Although the local economy was often very prosperous because of the docks, this was a fragile prosperity because of the casual and precarious nature of employment in the docks, with the area being struck by periods of severe recession during the nineteenth century. Even when this occasional prosperity did appear, it was unevenly distributed among the local population. Until 1967 labour in the docks was hired on a casual daily basis and that had the effect of keeping wage rates low and inculcating a culture of competition between individuals and working class communities. As in Middlesbrough, housing in the borough was constructed around the major sources of employment, often at the behest of the dock companies, but the employment available was much more fragmented, poorly paid, and uncertain. This not only contributed to the prevalence of poverty throughout the London Docks, but has, until recently, continued to affect the attitudes of the local population towards work. As Foster notes,

> The casual system had become so ingrained in people's thinking about dock work that it was not simply the employers who allowed it to continue for so long but the dockers themselves had 'a fatalistic acceptance of the system', believing that the nature of the work required, as employers' argued, 'the need for a margin of surplus labour to be hired or fired according to fluctuations in trade'. Even after casual labour was abolished, the hardships created by the system and the alienation of the workers subjected to it, remained in the form of a pervasive negativity and hostility among many local people through to the 1990s.
>
> (1999: 15, quoting Hill)

Following the Second World War the docks benefited from the boom in the UK national economy and levels of poverty in the East End of London as a whole fell. However, when structural decline set in, starting in the mid 1960s, problems of local over-provision by the dock companies, low levels of profitability, and general world-wide over-capacity in the shipping industry ensured that it was steep. By 1981 there were only 4100 dock workers employed in the London yards, down from 25,000 in 1960, a fall compounded by the decline in the many other local industries dependent on supplying the docks (Foster 1999: 41).

Efforts to rebuild the economy of the East End, and particularly that of

Docklands, began even before the docks finally closed, with a succession of 'dreams and schemes' being imposed on the area from the early 1970s (Foster 1999: 47). From the outset, however, many of the proposals recognised that the proximity of such a large area of real estate to the centre of London, and in particular the Square Mile of the City, offered a unique set of opportunities for a property-led regeneration strategy. The culmination of this process was the formation in 1981 of the London Docklands Development Corporation (LDDC) which was given sweeping powers to circumvent planning regulations and award tax and rates concessions in order to redevelop the docks as a site for international business and private sector housing. The creation of the LDDC created a new set of problems for a number of East End boroughs, including Tower Hamlets, which fell only partially within LDDC boundaries. In Tower Hamlets, the planning powers of the LDDC split the north of the borough, under the control of the local authority, from the south, including the very poor Isle of Dogs, which came under the LDDC. In economic terms the divisions created by the LDDC were far-reaching. Although the LDDC was nominally responsible for the development of the entire area and its resident population, in practice development activities were focused almost exclusively on the creation of office space for City firms and very expensive waterside housing developments for their employees. The early years of the LDDC's operations were marked by a speculative property boom. The ensuing frenzy of speculative development failed to take the interests of local residents into account, or benefit them in any significant way (the LDDC did nothing to improve the very dilapidated state of local social housing, for example). The recessions of the late 1980s had an immediate impact on the speculative developments in Docklands, many of which collapsed as over-inflated property prices plummeted. As the first wave of investors was swept away, however, the second and third waves – those that would build the more lasting developments such as Canary Wharf – were moving in to capitalise on the potential that was again being opened up (Foster 1999), but once again, ignoring the economic and social needs of local residents. The one or two attempts by the LDDC to fund community and housing projects were dwarfed by the wholesale transformation of the local economy brought about by major infrastructural investment to attract new private sector businesses.

The economic context of the social economy in Bristol and Tower Hamlets, therefore, has been marked first by high levels of disparity within and between local communities, and second by poverty in both places existing in close proximity to areas of prosperity. These characteristics have had an important formative influence upon the character and dynamics of the social economy there.

The geography of social exclusion

In Bristol there are some pockets of very severe and persistent deprivation among those areas and communities that have been excluded from the overall success of the 'sunbelt city'. As we noted above, these take two main forms: inner-city, predominantly ethnic minority, communities; large peripheral housing estates, particularly to the south of the city.

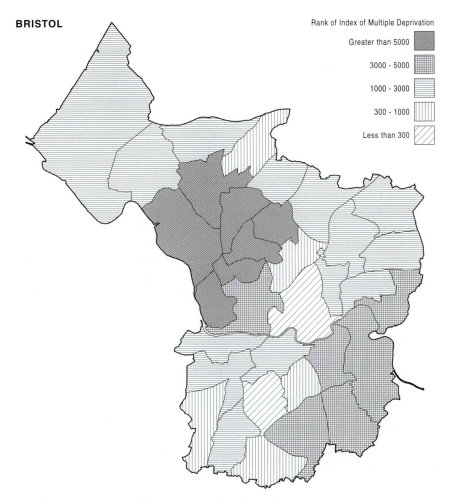

Figure 5.2 Index of Multiple Deprivation (IMD) map of Bristol.[2]

The problems of the inner-city areas of Bristol were graphically highlighted following the riots which swept through the St Pauls area in the early 1980s. Following the riots greater attention was paid to the area and a number of schemes was put in place, including several social economy organisations to attempt to tackle the worst of the problems. Although much has been achieved, the inner-city still has pockets of extreme poverty and exclusion which have remained largely unaffected because regeneration policies were either under-funded and short-term or oriented towards attracting major private sector investors. Although no area of Bristol ranks as highly across the aggregated indicators of deprivation as many of the wards in Glasgow, Middlesbrough, and Tower Hamlets, four outer-city wards – Filwood, Bishopswood, Knowle, and Hartcliffe – rank among the worst 100 areas for education deprivation in the UK (Filwood is the 7th most deprived). All four of these wards are adjoining, spread across the large housing estates to the south of Bristol which used to provide labour for the Wills Factory and other industrial sites. Inner-city areas such as Lawrence Hill, which ranks 133rd in the aggregate deprivation ranking for the UK, suffer from more general forms of multiple deprivation. Lawrence Hill lies to the east of the city centre and contains many of Bristol's ethnic minority communities.

Tower Hamlets, in contrast, is commonly regarded as one of the most deprived inner-city areas in Europe, despite years of regeneration effort. Five of its wards come within the most deprived 100 in the UK. These are concentrated on the main centres of the Bangladeshi community, particularly in Spitalfields, but also include some of the more traditional working class communities such as Blackwall on the Isle of Dogs. Spitalfields, for example, has the poorest housing in the UK and Blackwall one of the highest rates of child poverty. Both wards have some of the lowest levels of income in Britain. Poor housing is also a feature of most of the borough's other wards. Although Tower Hamlet's wards are within close physical

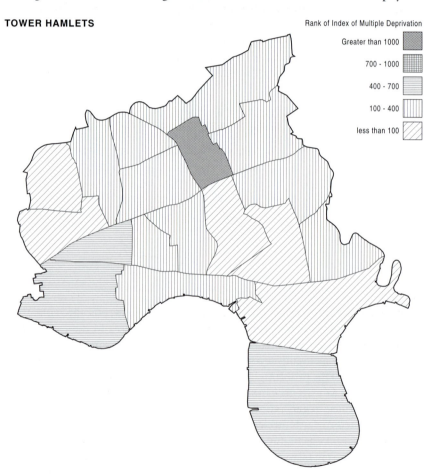

Figure 5.3 Index of Multiple Deprivation (IMD) map of Tower Hamlets.[2]

proximity to parts of London's prosperous economy, the Index of Multiple Deprivation (IMD) rankings on employment reveals a gulf in terms of social distance between the residents of Tower Hamlets and the surrounding buoyant labour market. Again it is the predominantly Bangladeshi wards that have the highest concentrations of unemployment, but throughout the rest of the borough the situation is comparable to that in Middlesbrough and, in some cases, worse.

The nature and scale of deprivation in Bristol and Tower Hamlets, therefore, is very different (see Figures 5.2 and 5.3). Bristol's problems may be long-standing and intractable, but they are at least identifiable and localised. In addition, they exist within the context of an area with a strong civic tradition of alterity and dissent (which we discuss below), much of which has been focused on issues of community and poverty. The situation in Tower Hamlets is different. With poverty and exclusion endemic across an array of fragmented and often hostile or defensive ethnically-defined communities, the complexity and magnitude of the task facing the social economy is that much greater. Despite this, by virtue of its location within the wider context of London, and in part because of the long tradition of welfare innovation in the borough, social economy organisations have none the less developed in Tower Hamlets. They are, however, as we see below, located in a divided civic and political culture marked by interest preservation and competition.

Civic resources

As noted above, the traditional working patterns of the London Docks left an enduring mark on the local community. Although they produced in many cases a strong sense of community centred on the shared identities of the working culture of the East End and the docks, in some parts of the area they also produced very insular and conservative forms of community. This became increasingly marked during the 1970s and 1980s when employment opportunities were beginning to dry up in the area and there were large influxes of refugees from the Indian sub-continent, particularly from Bangladesh, and latterly from parts of Africa, particularly Somalia. Immigration was not, however, new. The East End in general and Tower Hamlets in particular had long been host to ethnic minority communities (for example, the Huguenots in the eighteenth century, the large ethnic Chinese population of Limehouse and the Jewish immigrant communities in Stepney and Whitechapel during the nineteenth and twentieth centuries). However, so long as local employment was secure, and so long as such communities remained relatively small and contained, they were not perceived as a threat. As the scale of the influx into parts of Tower Hamlets during the 1970s increased and as ethnic minority families began to be placed in social housing in parts of the borough which had formerly been exclusively white, there was, however, a strong racist backlash (Foster 1999: 249). Parts of the Isle of Dogs and the east of the borough, which still contain large, predominantly white populations, produced particular hostility, with one ward on the Isle of Dogs briefly electing Britain's only British National Party (BNP) councillor on an openly racist platform in 1993 (Eade 1997). The short-lived success of the BNP represents the more extreme end of racism in local politics. Nevertheless, there is some evidence that other, more mainstream political parties in the borough were also deploying race as a means of garnering support in certain wards. The result of these various processes was to reinforce social division and insularity among the various ethnic groups that reside in Tower Hamlets.

The Bangladeshi community, for example, partly because of its own cultural needs, partly because of a genuine need for self-protection, and partly because of racialised housing allocations, formed a majority of the population around Spitalfields and Whitechapel, now often referred to as 'Banglatown' (Eade 1997). In 1991 the Bangladeshi community comprised 61 per cent of the local population in Spitalfields but only 4 per cent and 5 per cent, respectively, of the populations of Millwall on the Isle of Dogs and Bow on the eastern fringe (figures cited in Eade 1997). Other Bangladeshi communities also developed in estates to the north of the borough alongside existing white and Afro-Caribbean populations, latterly joined by Somali, Vietnamese, and other ethnic minority communities. There is, therefore, a particular ethnic geography within Tower Hamlets that is a product of successive waves of immigration, housing policies, and practices of resistance and discrimination. The differing needs of the various communities spread across the borough have contributed to the local Third Sector having distinctive differences between areas and communities. The insularity of many communities has created in some, notably parts of the Bengali and Somali communities, a degree of self-reliance that has provided fertile ground for the development of Third Sector activities. The Spitalfields Small Business Association and Account 3 projects detailed below, for example, have both developed successful niche markets for the Third Sector within ethnic minority communities. These have not necessarily grown out of the capacities of the communities themselves, but the communities do provide opportunities for outsiders to mobilise capacities within them to develop organisations that meet the targeted needs of local people. The communities that have proved more resistant to the development of local capacity have been the estates to the east of the borough. In these places of traditional white working class culture, there is a pervasive dependence upon local authority welfare provision.

In addition to the various working class and ethnic minority communities within Tower Hamlets, other groups have developed a significant presence in the area that is reflected in some of the activities of the social economy. Tower Hamlets is, along with Hackney to the north, reputed to have the highest concentration of visual artists of any comparable urban area in Europe. The effect of this on local civil society has been very varied. On the one hand some of the wealthier elements of the artistic community in the borough have contributed to particular forms of gentrification. Certain streets and squares have become almost entirely populated by artists and their studios (the best known of these is Beck Road in Hackney which has been largely occupied by artists since the 1970s). In Tower Hamlets many of the former dockyard buildings and empty wharves, especially around Limehouse and Wapping, were occupied by artists' studios prior to their redevelopment for housing and offices during the 1980s and 1990s. While the presence of these groups has never been as exclusionary as the more conventional forms of gentrification, the extent to which they have become integrated with other elements of the community has been varied. One of the main sources of interaction has been through some of the many outreach programmes run by local arts organisations. The Whitechapel Gallery at Aldgate East was established, along with a neighbouring library, in the 1890s as an educational establishment for the poor of the East End, and has been particularly important in forging such connections. These outreach programmes, whether organised through large organisations such as the Whitechapel or more informally, as in the case of the early stages of the Bromley-by-Bow project (p. 112) have often overlapped with the Third Sector, for example, through artists providing innovative arts-based training programmes. The Whitechapel Gallery runs a number of community-based education and outreach programmes which place artists, writers, and other creative workers in local schools and community centres. The Gallery works in association with local arts groups throughout Tower Hamlets and the East End more generally. Much of its work is concerned with inner-city problems and their exploration through the creative arts.[3] As in the case of the Bromley-by-Bow Centre, visual artists have been involved in social economy and voluntary sector projects, in this case providing arts classes for people with learning disabilities and other mental health problems in exchange for studio space.

The association between Tower Hamlets and innovation in the voluntary sector is well-established, with a very long history, a reflection of the long history of poverty and inequality in the area. Toynbee Hall, which still operates as a voluntary sector centre in the borough, was the first 'university settlement' in the UK established in Whitechapel in the 1884. This, and other inner-city missions (such as the Whitechapel Mission set up in 1876)[4] were philanthropic church-based organisations committed to the improvement and relief of the poor and dispossessed of the East End, a role they continue to perform. By pioneering services such as free legal advice and other social experiments, organisations such as Toynbee Hall prefigured many aspects of the post-war welfare state. They also served as a focal point for people wishing to help the inner-city poor, often for religious or political reasons, who came into the borough to work with local communities. It is partly because of this history that the recently established School for Social Entrepreneurs has been established in Tower Hamlets at Bethnal Green.

Poverty has been and is pervasive among almost all the various communities that constitute the long-resident elements of the local population in Tower Hamlets, producing a strong sense of competition for influence, resources, and territory. The middle classes that have been moving into Tower Hamlets since the early 1980s have been from elsewhere and have indirectly caused the displacement of poor people and communities. It is also the case that the pervasive poverty of the borough has meant that Third Sector organisations that have been able to develop have done so through the efforts of people from outside the borough who are committed to community-based regeneration (for religious, political or cultural reasons). This is in part a consequence of the fact that social economy networks in London have long transcended the political boundaries of individual boroughs and, indeed, have recently been formalised as Social Enterprise London

(SEL), in large part through the efforts of Tower Hamlets-based activists.

The character of civil society in Bristol, although to a degree also fragmented along social and ethnic lines, is very different to that of Tower Hamlets. Undoubtedly, there is poverty in Bristol but it occurs on a much smaller and more localised scale than in Tower Hamlets. Consequently, in Bristol, the relatively small pockets of poverty within the inner-city and the peripheral housing estates have a different relationship to the social whole. People may be poor and marginal, but they are nevertheless seen to be part of a wider social and political entity, which includes different social classes, ethnic identities, and territorial communities. This implies that while there may be differences between the many social and ethnic groups that constitute Bristol, there is also a sense of common identity, however minimal. This gives people a sense of belonging to the city in a way not possible in a place such as Tower Hamlets which is part of a much larger metropolitan area.

Bristol is also recognised as a place of cultural alterity. One social economy activist attributed this sense of alterity and willingness to experiment to Bristol's 'yeoman spirit'.[5] More generally, it can be linked to the long association of the city with alternative lifestyles, cultures, and politics. In religious terms, for example, Bristol has long been a centre of dissenting Christian cultures, both in the form of the powerful Quaker families which dominated the confectionery industry in the city and as a centre of Methodism.[6] Both the Quakers and Methodists have strong traditions of social involvement and anti-poverty activity and, particularly in the latter case, have recently had direct involvement in the promotion and development of Third Sector activities. Partly related to this history of religious dissent, Bristol also has a strong tradition of environmental activism, which again has been instrumental in developing some of the more vigorous local social enterprises. The Bristol Green Party was established in 1975 as the People's Party, later becoming the Ecology Party before taking on its current identity. The Bristol Green Party is now divided into three linked parties covering different areas of the city.[7] Bristol is home to one of the largest and longest established Friends of the Earth (FoE) groups in the UK, which has enjoyed strong support from people throughout the city from the early 1970s. Since the establishment of the FoE office in Bristol in 1971, the organisation has been involved in several projects that can be seen as precursors to current social economy activities. Many of these projects were based on materials recycling and the reduction of energy consumption, replacing services withdrawn by the council. Some of these, particularly a project which used money from recycling to provide insulation for elderly people and provide youth training, predate some of the better-known social enterprises, such as the Wise Group, by some years.[8]

Political culture

In both Middlesbrough and Glasgow a strong corporatist political culture has had a direct impact on the development of Third Sector activities. Even though the outcomes in terms of the form, character, and vitality of their social economies are very different, in both places local government is pivotally involved. In contrast, the picture in Bristol and Tower Hamlets is one of more distributed capacity and a much less state-centred social economy. This is a consequence of the ways in which the different actors within each place have come to influence local political practices and, as a consequence, to affect the nature of the relationship between the state, civil society, and the social economy.

Tower Hamlets has long been marked by a fragmented political culture. On occasion, this has been exacerbated by institutional and policy changes. The creation of the LDDC, for example, bifurcated political control over significant aspects of the borough and effectively denied the population of the Docklands areas, particularly the Isle of Dogs, the same degree of political accountability and dialogue available outside the LDDC-controlled area (Foster 1999). Tower Hamlets Council was still responsible for the provision of services within the LDDC area, particularly in the form of the existing provision of social housing, but in practice did little for these communities for the first few years of the LDDC's existence. In any event it had no powers to veto the planning decisions taken by the development corporation, regardless of the views of local residents. The construction of Canary Wharf, for example, was vehemently opposed by local people but their views were simply disregarded as the decision to proceed with the scheme was taken (Foster 1999).

The ethnic diversity of the borough too has had an important impact on the nature of local politics, particularly as sections of the Bangladeshi community have grown in influence. At various times the balance of power between the main parties competing for control of the borough council (which, in Tower Hamlets, is between Labour and the Liberal Democrats) has been held by a small group of Bangladeshi councillors whose allegiance has been actively sought over various contentious issues. Given the racial tensions that have long been a feature of the local civil society, this is perceived by some as giving some parts of the borough and their communities a disproportionate influence in policy decisions.[9] Allegations of corruption among a small minority of these councillors have only heightened these tensions. The racial dimension to the political culture in Tower Hamlets and other areas of East London has had, according to Eade, profound consequences:

> Different scapes have been created as these localities have become increasingly economically, socially and culturally both heterogeneous and highly fragmented. Despite the sharp disparities in wealth which have emerged in London's East End this heterogeneity has so far produced a situation where unequal social actors have looked past each other and kept their (social) distance. Conflict has usually occurred around a racialized boundary between working class whites and their Bangladeshi neighbours. The globalization of locality in Docklands and Spitalfields has not produced a new politics of place where social and cultural differences can be accommodated within a strategy of working-class resistance.
>
> (1997: 144)

Eade's contention that the encroachment of global forces into Tower Hamlets has not produced a new politics of place is important. It does not support claims about the emergence of a new and progressive 'global sense of place' in sites of cosmopolitan mixture (Massey 1991). What we find in Tower Hamlets is a defensive and regressive politics of turf, often mobilised through strong diasporic or other connections of closed cultural ties.

Bristol's strong tradition of civic and environmental activism, in contrast, has fed into a more inclusive, albeit demarcated, politics of place. For it is important to distinguish between the place politics of the city council and those of local and community political activists, with important consequences for the development of the local social economy. As one current Third Sector activist in Bristol put it:

> There is no real commitment to the social economy outside of the sector itself. The local authority does have a political voice loud enough to get the message out that this is an opportunity and that this is going to be the culture of the city. But it is not going to be the culture of the city because it is not even the culture of the local authority. It is probably more the culture of the citizens of Bristol than it is of the local authority.[10]

Until very recently Bristol City Council has avoided direct involvement in non-mainstream regeneration strategies. The unwillingness of the entrenched Labour establishment in Bristol to be dictated, during the 1980s and early 1990s, by the Conservative government (Malpass 1994) led to the rejection of the inner-city regeneration schemes introduced by the Conservatives. Ironically this refusal to engage in mainstream regeneration activities is in part a consequence of the culture of dissent and independence that has produced a strong civic base for the social economy. This 'municipalism', however, has fallen well short of 'radical' development strategies, including, until quite recently, the encouragement of community enterprises:

> Most of Bristol's policies have . . . fitted within the traditional type of strategy, involving a heavy reliance on site assembly, support for small firms and promotional activities [. . .] The guiding of investment to areas of high unemployment, and the targeting of job creation towards particularly vulnerable groups, has tended to be a secondary objective . . . many of the workshops and small firm projects in inner-city areas have been small in scale and are best characterized as 'mopping up' policies, easing the impacts of decline rather than laying the basis for economic regeneration. . . .
>
> (Boddy *et al.* 1986: 196–7)

This rather bleak analysis of the situation in the late 1980s led Boddy *et al.* to the conclusion that the role of locally-based regeneration strategies in Bristol, such as they were, had been of scarcely any importance in addressing the needs of the city's poor and marginal communities.

... no specific urban or regional policy measures, central or local, are heavily implicated in the particular processes of economic and employment change [in Bristol]. . . . There are examples of innovative and, at the local scale, effective initiatives from which lessons can be drawn. Their impact in overall economic and employment terms, however, has been essentially irrelevant.

(op. cit.: 213)

Bristol's reticence to develop active regeneration programmes for the city's poor and marginal communities has been compounded, until very recently, by an inability to bid for the sort of mainstream regeneration funds that have contributed to the development of social economy activities in other cities. Because of its relative overall wealth, Bristol was also often not eligible for particular regeneration funds, notwithstanding acute problems in inner-city and peripheral wards. When the local authority did finally begin to apply for such funds, Bristol notoriously failed to win money from two successive City Challenge rounds (Punter 1993). More recent bids have been more successful, helped in part by a change in the make-up of the City Council and an influx of younger officers and councillors, particularly following the abolition of Avon County in 1996 and the restoration of Bristol City Council as a unitary authority.

The election in 1997, however, of George Micklewright (a former officer with the Bristol Co-operative Development Agency) as Leader of the City Council marked a significant change in the Council's attitude towards the Third Sector. This was partly a consequence of Micklewright's personal commitment to community-based economic development and partly because it was becoming increasingly evident that local social enterprises in Bristol were far from irrelevant by the late 1990s. Shortly after taking office, at a workshop organised by the Bristol Area Community Enterprise Network (BACEN), Micklewright asserted his belief in the role of the social economy at both local and national levels and announced his intention to make its development a key theme of his leadership. This led to the establishment of a three-year, £400,000 evaluation project, headed by a social economy activist seconded into the Council's regeneration team. This project had two main aims: first, to assess the current extent and effectiveness of the Third Sector in the city; second, to identify possible ways in which the local authority could help it to develop further. This marked a watershed in the attitude of the local authority towards the social economy.

The social economy in Bristol

Despite the common expectation that the social economy flourishes in areas of marked social exclusion, paradoxically, of our four case areas, the prosperous city of Bristol has the most extensive and successful social economy. A recent survey of the local social economy conducted by Bristol City Council generated over 400 completed questionnaires from organisations throughout the city. Although only 17 per cent of these were social enterprises in the strict sense, this nevertheless implies a high level of Third Sector activity relative to the scale of need (in sharp contrast, for example, to the low level in Middlesbrough). In addition to a significant number of community-based organisations spread throughout the city, including social enterprises, some of which we examine in greater detail below, Bristol is also host to several national charities and environmental organisations, many of which are involved in aspects of social economy development on a national scale. These include the Single Parent Action Network, the National Federation of City Farms, the Soil Association, and Sustrans. Bristol also houses the UK headquarters of such organisations as the Dutch-founded Triodos Bank, an ethical bank which in addition to offering a range of banking services supports social and environmental improvement projects.[11] The presence of such organisations helps create a supportive context for social economy initiatives and experiments.

Since the late 1970s, several social enterprises operating on a city-wide scale have developed based on the well-established environmental movements in the Bristol area. The most notable of these were established by FoE in association with Avon County Council. More generally, they have gradually developed into effective, self-sustaining social enterprises that have become firmly established as part of local anti-poverty strategies as well as influential elements in the local social economy as a whole. They also incorporate organisational principles based on altruism, equality, and equity, in strong contrast to firms in the mainstream economy. In this way, they help reproduce diversity and the exploration of alternative social relations to those of the mainstream economy. The SOFA[12] and Children's Scrapstore projects, both of which are members of the wider Bristol Recycling Consortium, exemplify many of the features of these organisations.

The SOFA project was founded with the help of FoE and the County Council in 1980 by two committed Christians to recycle and renovate second-hand furniture for resale to people on low incomes and living in poor-quality social housing. The purpose of SOFA was from the outset to combine the provision of environmentally friendly social services – reducing landfill and providing affordable furnishing for those on low incomes – with job creation and training. SOFA operates a transport network that collects used furniture and white goods throughout the city for refurbishment in its workshop and resale through its warehouse. At the time of writing, the warehouse itself was undergoing a £1.5 million refurbishment to provide purpose-built workshops and office space, situated in a run-down shopping street to the east of the city centre. In addition to expanding SOFA's own workshop and retail space, the new building will contain office space to be rented to other social enterprises working in the area. The long-term aim is to create a largely self-funding centre, a social economy 'one stop shop', in which a range of services, including SOFA, health-care, employment advice, and a credit-union are available in the same place. The project hopes that, by bringing clients, and ultimately tenants of the workspaces, into the area, other local businesses will benefit from increased spending and investment.

SOFA in 2000 employed fourteen people, and had a core of professional staff that ran the social enterprise with very tight financial management and a business-like approach. SOFA would not survive were it to pay staff, particularly the senior management, private sector equivalent wages (one reason why, as noted in Chapter 2, wage rates in the social economy more generally tend to be lower than private sector equivalents). The director of the project is not originally from Bristol, and could well find a better paid job in the private sector. However, his ethics, his network links in the Bristol social economy, and the personal satisfaction he derives from working with the local community, have kept him in the sector – one form of effective place ties in the social economy.

This type of local commitment is perhaps even more evident in another project established by FoE and Avon Council in 1982. Like SOFA, the Children's Scrapstore was established to combine ecological objectives (in this case, reductions in land-fill waste) with socially useful services and employment. Scrapstore collects clean scrap from local businesses – paper, textiles, plastics, cardboard tubes, and so on – which otherwise would be discarded. The materials collected are sorted in a warehouse and then resold, at very low cost, to child-care organisations throughout the Bristol area for use as art materials. To extend its revenue potential, Scrapstore opened part of its floorspace as a conventional retail art shop, selling a variety of proprietary paints, glues, tools, and other materials and equipment both to its members (the child-care organisations) and to the general public, but often at subsidised prices. Scrapstore has developed into one of the biggest social economy organisations of its type in the UK and is able to generate sufficient revenue to cover over 60 per cent of its £250,000 per annum running costs. A proposed move in 2000 to a new building, which the project would buy outright with the help of charitable donations and a mortgage, would remove some of the restrictions that currently constrain its ability to develop further revenue streams.

Like SOFA, the Scrapstore staff earn less than they would in the private sector. Instead, they have chosen to become involved in this workers' collective.[13] Unlike a co-operative, which can operate as a normal private sector business except that it is owned by some of its employees, a workers' collective is owned in equal share by all of its employees. Furthermore, it is managed democratically and all employees are paid the same wage regardless of the task they perform. Scrapstore's seven full-time staff (in 1999/2000) come from all walks of life and are employed as much for their willingness to adhere to the principles of the collective as for their individual skills. Like SOFA, the motivation is less financial than that of job satisfaction, a personal commitment to a particular form of democratic enterprise, and response to a local need.

Based on a different kind of commitment – Christian Methodism – Aspire Community Enterprise Ltd was established in 1998 by two young men to create employment opportunities for homeless people in the city. Homeless clients deliver a catalogue to areas of the city, advertising products from 'fair-trade' and/or renewable sources, including greetings cards, candles, ornaments, gifts, and jewellery. Aspire's 'employees' call at houses to collect orders or unwanted catalogues, and to deliver goods purchased. Profits are ploughed back into the

Plate 5.1 Bristol, Children's Scrapstore.

project. The purpose of Aspire is to give homeless people a sense of belonging and purpose as well as income and work training. Although Aspire will take on anyone regardless of their personal history, which often involves drug and/or alcohol abuse and other offences, clients are expected to be punctual and sober when carrying out their work for the project. No attempt is made to proselytise, though project leaders are explicit in their desire to demonstrate the foundations of their faith by example. Aspire also, however, has the aim of educating the general public about homeless people, much in the same way that Gabalfa (discussed in Chapter 3) does with regard to people with learning disabilities, by breaking down barriers and bringing people into direct contact.

All three of these projects have become or are becoming (Aspire) established social enterprises. All three derive their success as social enterprises from a combination of the particular niche markets they have identified, the availability of funding, even if only to establish the project, but above all the personal

Plate 5.2 Bristol, new private sector housing opposite Scrapstore.

commitment of the individuals running them. Importantly, none of these projects are neighbourhood or community-based, in the sense that they are owned by or operate solely within a particular area of Bristol (all have a city-wide remit). Rather, they rely on the capacity of committed and skilled people willing to work for relatively low wages (and/or able to absorb low wages) to establish services which are then made available to the excluded. Significantly, this commitment underpins a form of social enterprise that bears only a passing resemblance to a concept of social enterprise as the spontaneous product of poor people developing latent capacities in poor places. If place matters, here it is as a site of professional and ethical commitment.

There is also, however, some, albeit rare, evidence of grass-roots activism. South Bristol Community Builders Ltd, for example, was established in 1998 to redevelop run-down and empty council houses on the Knowle estate in the south of Bristol. Knowle is a large, sprawling low rise estate built mainly in the 1940s and 1950s to provide housing for workers in the tobacco and manufacturing industries. Knowle's problems are particularly those associated with crime and drug abuse, which is rife on the estate, and with the gradual depopulation of the estate, which has left empty houses that are squatted and/or vandalised. South Bristol Community Builders was established by the wife of a local builder, to upgrade the local housing stock. Using her own savings, and with the help of other local women, she purchased and refurbished (with the help of her husband builder) a house on the estate, which was then put on the market and sold. Proceeds from sales are being used to develop other properties. This social entrepreneur has been responsible for developing other projects in the past, including an anti-drug abuse project run by local women, local health provision, and more generally with activities aimed at generating a positive image for the area. In this case the enthusiasm and commitment is born of a stubborn belief in the local community and a desire to restore to it a sense of pride in place. Place clearly matters in this case as a site of attachment, commitment, and social obligation.

A similar sense of community obligation can be found in two other projects, both of which were established primarily to meet the particular needs of Bristol's ethnic minority groups in the inner-city. The Aashyana Housing Association was founded in 1992 after research carried out by local Asian community and business leaders demonstrated that available housing was often too small for traditional extended families or was too far from friends, family, and other members of the Asian community. Many Asian people in the area were found to be living in poor or overcrowded housing and had difficulties finding appropriate help and advice. Language problems and alleged discrimination on the part of some local housing associations compounded these problems. Aashyana offers housing advice in Hindi, Urdu, and Punjabi, as well as English, and manages a much wider range of property types than most housing associations, so that it can accommodate both single people of all ages and, where necessary, large, extended families. As it developed, Aashyana commissioned further research from the University of the West of England into the housing conditions of the local Asian community. The research showed that the approximately 8000 people of Asian descent, living in sixteen wards in Bristol and three in South Gloucestershire, were in areas that suffered a disproportionately high incidence of housing problems, ill-health, and low income compared to the general population. Aashyana has been able to use such information both to target its existing services and to demonstrate to funders the continued need for the project. Aashyana in 2000 managed thirty-one homes for general clients, five more specifically for young single people, and four purpose-built flats for Asian elders – the first scheme of its kind in the South-West of England. A further twenty-four homes had been renovated and transferred to Aashyana from the City Council and there were plans for further expansion through the transfer of management of dwellings to Aashyana from local housing associations. Somewhat unusually, Aashyana has become largely independent of external funding for its running costs, which are generated through rents from its clients. The City Council agreement gives Aashyana the collateral for loans to buy and renovate or build more homes for the Asian community. Aashyana's success lies in the combination of its director's professional capabilities, coupled to the support it receives among 'elders' within the community it serves, and its power of leverage over other key players such as the City Council.

The second example rooted in target community commitment (but perhaps with less input from the community itself at the level of resources) is the St Pauls-based Centre for Employment and Enterprise Development (CEED). CEED was founded in 1987 as one of thirteen Positive Action Training for Housing (PATH) schemes throughout the UK which were established to provide training for housing officers in the needs of ethnic minority communities. While the Bristol PATH project was successful in meeting its targets, subsequent evaluation of the project concluded that its aims were too limited. In 1990 it was renamed as the Positive Action Consortium and appointed its first director, who until then had been running a successful community enterprise in Toxteth on Merseyside. The renamed organisation extended the principle of Positive Action training from housing to all business sectors, offering training courses to employers throughout the Bristol area as well as to individuals within the immediate community. Renamed as CEED in 1995, under its charismatic and entrepreneurial director, the project has developed and grown, to cover a variety of training needs and work-experience opportunities (e.g. in its media unit and restaurant). CEED has moved from being 100 per cent dependent on grant funding in 1982 to obtaining only 2 per cent income in the form of grants in 2000. The bulk of its income comes in the form of fees, rents, and service contracts and it generates an annual surplus of as much as £170,000 (1999) all of which, as a community enterprise, is ploughed back into provision of services. Like Aashyana, CEED is unusual in its capacity to fund its activities in this way.

Although the vast majority of CEED's clients are from the local Afro-Caribbean community, the project director is convinced that the success of CEED is rooted in its professional approach as a high quality enterprise. A fundamental aspect of CEED's approach is to treat all members of the client community, regardless of their background, as having particular needs and capacities in terms of business development and expansion, rather than as 'special cases' or 'victims'. In similar fashion, CEED itself is therefore keen to be held up as an example of a good business, rather than labelled as a good 'ethnic minority' business. CEED's director is also somewhat dismissive of other social enterprises in Bristol, includ-ing those in the black community, that fail to develop through entrepreneurship and sustained growth and promote themselves as fundamentally different from the private and/or public sectors. In his own words:

> Whether people fully understand the concept of the social enterprise is another thing. I personally don't think they do. My opinion is that any voluntary sector organisation *must* operate along business lines. The only difference between a social enterprise and normal enterprise is simply that there are no shareholders that receive a dividend, but there are 'shareholders' in terms of the members and the community at large who may benefit from the initiatives that are put together. [. . .] have to say that I don't meet

members of the voluntary sector in smoke filled rooms myself . . . primarily because it is not other voluntary sector organisations that can enable me to achieve what I want to achieve. It is in linking with the private sector and the statutory sector and raising their awareness levels to such an extent that I am able to persuade them to support what we are doing.[14]

While CEED stands as an example of an extraordinarily successful social enterprise in Bristol, therefore, it also represents something of a challenge to the image of the Third Sector as a radical alternative. CEED does not seek to create an alternative to capitalism – quite the opposite. What CEED seeks to demonstrate is that anyone, regardless of their ethnic background, gender, or postcode can develop successful careers, given the appropriate level of training and support. As such, it raises important questions as to how 'success' is to be defined and about the factors that underpin success.

As much as this turns the notion of the social economy on its head, it also suggests something important about the particular reasons why so many social enterprises have been able to develop so successfully in Bristol. CEED's success in part can be attributed to its capacity to involve the private sector and, in turn, to combine private and public sector funds. CEED is able to tap Bristol's vibrant private sector economy for ideas, resources, partnerships, and new markets. Furthermore, the buoyancy of the local economy generates sufficient local labour-market capacity to absorb trained clients (assuming barriers of race and culture have been broken down) and start-up businesses. Indeed, for all the claims to alterity, many of Bristol's social enterprises also to some degree rely on the strength of the local mainstream economy for their survival.[15]

But there is more. A striking feature of the social economy in Bristol (notwithstanding the director of CEED's misgivings) is that it is well organised and networked (independently of the state). Bristol has a number of intermediate, networking and consultancy organisations established specifically by and for the support of the Third Sector. These include Voluntary Organisations Standing Conference on Urban Regeneration (VOSCUR), which provides networking and co-ordination for the Bristol voluntary sector as a whole, and BACEN, an SRB-funded project which provides start-up advice for community enterprises (defined in the strict sense) on a city-wide and potentially regional scale. These organisations in turn overlap with other networking bodies on a local and national level (most notably, FoE), the local authority and, to some extent, with the private sector. The result is a high degree of co-ordination, discussion, and debate among different organisations about the nature and role of the social economy as well as the routine dissemination of information as to best practice. This contrasts strikingly with the situation in Glasgow, where the social economy is managed not by the Third Sector itself, but by career professionals supported by the local state. This contrast was alluded to by the director of BACEN who, in 1998, had organised in a 'roving conference' including a range of social economy activists from the Bristol area, which travelled to Glasgow to learn from its the much vaunted success. As she put it:

The view from the outside was always that the Scots were very good at it, that there was a lot of expertise there, that it was very innovative, that it was very people led and so on. The people we took were from Hartcliffe and Withywood Ventures and a number of the other trusts in Bristol and community enterprises and voluntary organisations and so on. They were all really struck by the lack of [Third Sector] control. In some areas particularly in the north of Glasgow, they were also struck by the lack of community activism. . . . We were just meeting with these community partnership people which had no contact with the local people and they couldn't even wheel anyone in from the local community to meet us because they didn't know any of them. In every project or initiative that we went to see we met a professional, a man in a suit. We went to a health project in Castlemilk and we did meet some of the partners there but they were so depressed and disillusioned – completely disempowered.[16,17]

To be sure, social economy projects in Bristol are not necessarily community-owned or run by local people. Indeed, with the sole exception of South Bristol Community Builders, all the projects we studied in the area were run by middle class professionals who were delivering the social economy on behalf of local people. What then differentiates the professional social entrepreneur in Bristol from the 'man in a suit' in Glasgow? A significant part of the answer seems to lie in the nature of the relationship between the individuals involved and the communities in which they work. In Bristol the social economy is organised by middle class professionals who have chosen to work in and for the values of the social economy. In Glasgow there is a commitment on the part of the city council to the idea of business success in certain markets for 'social' goods. It is, in this sense, not rooted in the day-to-day realities of the communities in which the enterprises operate (not least because of the way funding is targeted). In Bristol the opposite is the case. Professionals who make the choice to work in the social economy do so because of their personal religious, political or environmental commitments. As such, the focus tends to be more one of how the social economy can serve the particular community than one of the community fitting into a particular model of business enterprise, as tends to happen in Glasgow.

The social economy in Tower Hamlets

The fragmented nature of economic, social, and political change in Tower Hamlets during recent decades has not unsurprisingly left its mark on the nature and distribution of the local social economy. The uneven geography of its various regeneration schemes has also influenced the location of Third Sector activity (Figure 5.4).[18] Given this degree of variability, it is problematic to conceptualise Tower Hamlets as a single and unified social economy. The different projects relate to local and non-local institutional structures, funding sources, communities and wider networks in very different ways. The examples below illustrate the widely differing conditions under which social enterprises in different parts of

CURRENT REGENERATION INITIATIVES IN LBTH

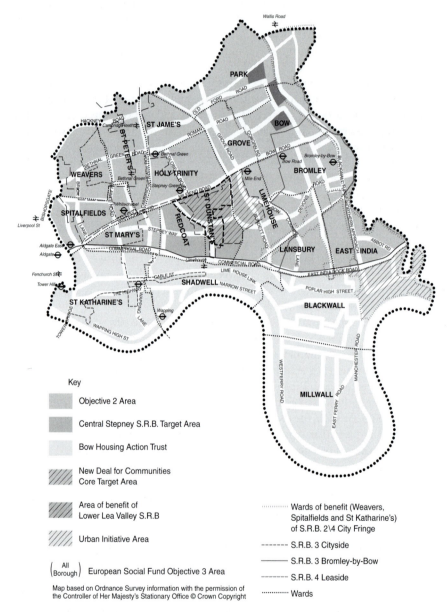

Figure 5.4 London Borough of Tower Hamlets regeneration scheme map.

the borough operate and the ways in which the social economy is shaped by this local context.

There are no data on the total number of social enterprises currently operating in Tower Hamlets. A very large number and varied range of voluntary sector organisations are present in the borough, ranging from small community centres and arts groups to long established organisations, such as the Whitechapel Mission and Toynbee Hall. However, there are relatively few genuine social enterprises. These include the Spitalfields Small Business Association (SSBA) and Bridge Project to the west of the borough, Account 3 which is based in St Margarets House[19] in Bethnal Green to the north, Poplar Housing and Regeneration Community Association (HARCA) and the Bromley-by-Bow Centre to the east, and the Cedar Centre on the Isle of Dogs. This relatively small number of social enterprises is to some extent a product of the scale on which they operate. All cover significant parts of the borough, are engaged in providing a range of services for local people, and absorb a large proportion of available funding. This affects the capacity of the borough to support large numbers of smaller, very local Third Sector organisations, which would have to compete with these for funds. In addition, the development of two large-scale regeneration partnerships led by the local authority and the private sector, the Cityside and Lea Valley projects, has had the effect of deterring smaller social enterprises lacking the resources to cover a larger scale of need. This is one reason why the chances of many new, smaller-scale Third Sector projects developing in Tower Hamlets (ironically, precisely the highly localised Third Sector organisations based in one 'neighbourhood' expected by many Third Sector promoters) are restricted.

The part of Tower Hamlets with the most acute problems of poverty and exclusion, however, namely Spitalfields and Whitechapel (Banglatown), is also the site of some of the borough's oldest and best established social enterprises. This is in large part a consequence of the conditions in which many of the immigrant communities coming into the area found themselves and which prompted concerned organisations and individuals to establish welfare and support organisations. The best known of these is the SSBA which was established in 1979 to improve housing conditions for the local Bengali community. SSBA was not established by members of the Bengali community itself, but by a small group of women who had been politically active, as councillors, officers, and activists throughout the East End of London for some years. SSBA was an expedient response to two related problems: first, the slum housing conditions of the Bengali community; and second, the terrible conditions in workshops established in the same buildings to make a living through making clothes, light engineering activities, printing, and so on. Although SSBA had originally intended to take over only the local housing, it found it in practice impossible to separate living and work spaces. But since the Housing Corporation was unwilling to cover resources to refurbish the workspaces, SSBA bought the properties and split the deeds between the housing and business units. The housing units were then leased to a specially established housing co-operative which could then, because these sections of the buildings were no longer of mixed use, apply for refurbishment grants. This left SSBA in possession of a large number of small business units, which it has gradually refurbished and leased to local firms as managed workspace. As the project has grown, SSBA has also come to offer a range of business development, training, and consultancy services. SSBA currently manages over 65,000 square feet of workspace, housing around sixty small and medium enterprises. By controlling rent rises carefully, SSBA has also insulated vulnerable local businesses from the very high rises in commercial rents in the area during the 1980s and 1990s.

Another project in the same area – the Bridge Project – has worked with SSBA and a number of other local agencies to target employment training at particular groups within the local community and to help them set up their own businesses. This project (so called because it was originally housed in the Shaftesbury Society-owned, 'Bridge House' which provides low-rent space for local charities and social enterprises) was formally incorporated in 1987, having been run on a wholly voluntary basis by a group of local Christians since 1982. At the outset the Project aimed to promote self-employment and business development among young people. After moving out of the Bridge House, the Project occupied the crypt of a local church in which it offered small amounts of workspace through a joint Community Service Volunteers and Employment Agency scheme. After 1988 the Project broadened its remit to include all people facing discrimination and exclusion, especially recent Somali refugees requiring language support and help with the bureaucratic process of seeking asylum in the UK. The Project has had considerable difficulty in securing long-term funds because refugees entering into this laudable initiative still leave with so few skills that achieving the minimum outputs in terms of qualifications and employment sought by funders has been very difficult. The Bridge Project gets no direct support from the borough council. Although its work has produced outputs considered successful in its own terms, and is certainly seen as such by its client group, the Bridge Project's viability is compromised by its precarious financial situation. Project leaders blame the culture of accountancy among funders, the competitive nature of funding in general, and the demarcated nature of local regeneration funding. For example, although the many of the Project's clients are housed within the Objective 2 funding area in Tower Hamlets, because the Project is situated on the other side of the road from the boundary, it has been unable to secure grants from that source. Although the Project would like to become a self-funding social enterprise, the very uneven playing field in which it operates makes it in practice impossible for it to develop sufficient capacity for that to happen.

Both SSBA and the Bridge Project highlight the significance of shifting local funding priorities for the success of social enterprises. Regeneration activity within Tower Hamlets has shifted from one area to the next, and from smaller to larger organisations. In both cases, and particularly in that of SSBA, relations between the project and the local authority are poor. This is also due to the complex and shifting political agenda of the council, which creates an uneven and uncertain funding regime. There is, for example, considerable pressure from the Bengali community which feels that it is represented neither by the conventional political establishment nor by its own, often self-appointed, representatives. While SSBA has been able to develop a secure asset base over the long period in which it has been operating, the Bridge Project, in spite of its success in developing new services and in securing short-term finance, finds itself unable to compete for funding with other social economy activities.

Elsewhere in the borough, other projects have in contrast benefited from the shifts in regeneration priorities. Of these, the largest and most successful has been Account 3 Women's Consultancy Service Ltd, established in 1991. Account 3 was set up by three professional women (an accountant, a personnel manager, and a marketing manager), all of whom had worked in the private sector and were at the time temporarily unemployed. Having come together originally as a self-help group on an informal basis, they began to identify the particular needs of local Somali women who were excluded from employment and other forms of social interaction by virtue of language difficulties, skills deficits, and cultural differences. With the support of the local authority, the women conducted a survey of women from the Somali and Bengali communities living on estates in Bethnal Green. This highlighted a marked need for English language education. Following this, the three women formalised the organisation as Account 3 and were awarded a contract to provide basic language education on the estates in question. In the process of providing this, it became apparent that the problems faced by the women were not confined to those of language, but also related to confidence, skills, and social and cultural capabilities.

In its second year of operation, therefore, Account 3 expanded its services to offer a range of structured courses, at varying levels and with flexible content, depending on the needs of the client group in question. These courses have continued to form the core of Account 3's activity. One of Account 3's more innovative and successful courses, for example, trains local women as driving instructors. For cultural and religious reasons many Somali women in particular were prevented from taking driving lessons because the instructor was usually male. By training local women as instructors in their own right, Account 3 has enabled many local women to gain access to the freedom accorded by driving as well as access to job opportunities outside the immediate area. In addition to these various skills training courses, Account 3 has developed a range of business support programmes which offer training in accountancy and marketing to small businesses and in 2000 it was planning to develop a workspace scheme to help long-term unemployed women to set up their own businesses.

Unlike the older projects in the east of the borough, the relationship between Account 3 and the local authority has been generally positive and supportive. Nearly all of Account 3's £500,000 annual turnover comes in the form of local authority contracts (it has avoided grants wherever possible) which, its founders believe, lends them credibility as a social enterprise. Account 3 has been able to develop close working relationships with council officers to whom it can go both to iron out problems and to develop new projects. Project leaders attribute their ability to do this in large part to their business-like approach to the organisation of the project, which is based on a realistic assessment of what they want to achieve and the best way to achieve it within available resources. Everything that Account 3 does is 'research led' so that it can demonstrate to funders that a real need and/or demand for project activities exists. This is distinctly different from the more politicised, activist approach of some of the older projects and reflects, as Account 3's leaders acknowledge, a generational difference. The link with the council, however, makes the organisation highly vulnerable to political changes within the council. As such Account 3 takes a deliberately entrepreneurial approach and has cultivated extensive private sector links through Women's Enterprise, as well as forging wider links with the Government Office for London.

The more recently established projects in Tower Hamlets are located to the east of the borough, in estates which have often been most resistant to outsiders, particularly ethnic minorities, and to 'outside' interference in the form of the voluntary sector. There are two major social economy projects in this part of Tower Hamlets, each generated by very different dynamics. The first we report is illustrative of a new state-led thrust to the social economy, and for that reason, contested. The second underscores the powers of possibility resulting from imaginative and energetic social entrepreneurs/professionals, network links beyond the locality, and a holistic approach to social exclusion.

The larger of the two, Poplar HARCA, was established in 1998. It was one of the first of a new generation of Third Sector housing associations set up to manage large areas of social housing that were passing out of the direct control of local authorities throughout the UK as part of the government's stock transfer scheme. The HARCA was established by the borough council as an independent social enterprise, which will eventually manage eleven blocks of housing containing over 7000 homes. It has a ten-year business plan and considerable resources (a combination of grants from the council and loans from a consortium of commercial banks) with which it will refurbish the estates under its control and develop a range of integrated and holistic social and environmental services. Many of these will be social enterprises in their own right, as the HARCA plans to develop estates as largely self-managed 'resident service organisations' (Saunders 1997) which will employ local people to carry out basic maintenance, cleaning, and security work. The HARCA has already established project offices in all the housing blocks it controls, each staffed by a development officer, and is using them to identify the particular needs of each estate.

Significantly, though, the establishment of Poplar HARCA has not been universally welcomed by the residents of the estates, despite a very long history of chronic under-investment and neglect by the local authority. As in other parts of the UK, a vociferous campaign has been fought by a section of the local community that is politically opposed to what it sees as 'privatisation'. Although investment is now being put into the estates and the HARCA rents are lower than those of the local authority, the campaign against the project has been sufficiently successful to prevent the transfer of a third tranche of housing.[20] The tradition of resistance to outside interference has also contributed to the HARCA's problems. Campaigners have argued that rents would rise very quickly as the project's private sector lenders called in their debts and that levels of maintenance and repair would fall. Paradoxically, although the HARCA's constitution stops either of these things from happening, a sufficiently large minority of the local community voted against the third phase of the transfer to prevent it. The HARCA is a good example of how top-down solutions, even excellent ones, are dependent on community endorsement for local viability.

The second major social economy project in the east of Tower Hamlets is the Bromley-by-Bow Centre which, although it originated in 1984, has only expanded relatively recently and gained national recognition.[21] The Centre was established by a local minister who offered space in his church hall to local artists who in turn offered art classes to residents of the surrounding estates and people with mental health problems. Over time new activities developed, including a day nursery, which occupies the main body of the church when it is not being used for services, a garden for people with disabilities, and a café. SRB money was raised to buy a neighbouring building which allowed space to expand the café into a restaurant run by members of the local Bengali community as a separate enterprise. This has given them a springboard to expand their business by providing outside catering services for functions throughout the area. The aspect of the project that has attracted the greatest attention, however, has been the integrated healthy living centre, which was built by the Centre in 1996. The health centre comprises a medical practice, housing four general practitioners (GPs) (intended to expand to six), with a range of other health and welfare services under the same roof. Patients visiting the doctors can also get advice on alternative remedies (such as acupuncture and aromatherapy), use the baby-care clinic, have access to healthy living advice (exercise is available on prescription), advice on diet (the project includes a kitchen to demonstrate healthy food), and have access to the gardens behind the centre which have been designed as a space for relaxation for local people. The health centre was built with a combination of a health authority grant and a £700,000 commercial loan and then 'sold' to Bromley-by-Bow itself for a token ninety-nine pence. The loans will be paid off over time by the GPs practice. Since the centre was built, Bromley-by-Bow has won another £200,000 grant with which it is developing a specially designed children's garden to the rear of the centre and is planning to buy a further building to house officespace and further projects.

The success of Bromley-by-Bow at developing innovative and integrated services for local people has been brought about as a result of local people working with Third Sector entrepreneurs from elsewhere. Bromley-by-Bow has been able to develop a very wide range of connections with other organisations, in large part through the efforts of some of its supporters and staff. One of the main participants in the development of the project, for example, is both a consultant surgeon at Guy's Hospital and a councillor in the neighbouring borough of Newham. This has not only influenced the health-oriented activities of the Centre but, through the various networks to which such individuals have access, it has facilitated some unlikely partnerships. The children's garden, for example, is part funded by the UK Atomic Energy Establishment at Aldermaston, which organised a visit by local school children to its laboratories, and helped them to design the various sculptural elements within the garden around the theme of

Plate 5.3 Bromley-by-Bow Centre's new café.

nuclear energy. Bromley-by-Bow has also benefited from seconded staff from the Ministry of Defence and from several other central government departments which has allowed the project to enhance its profile on a national basis. More recently, the Centre has been able to secure work placements for local people in firms in Canary Wharf, a development which project leaders feel demonstrates the beginnings of 'reciprocity' between local residents and the businesses that have come into the borough as part of the regeneration schemes.

The Centre's networking also extends deeply into the wider social economy of London. Its leaders were very influential, along with the Tower Hamlets Co-operative Development Agency and the borough's Community Organisations Forum, in establishing the pan-London body, SEL, in 1999. This new body, which has close links to the government, is intended to work closely with the new London Assembly to ensure that social economy issues are properly represented within the capital as a whole. This change represents a scale shift in the governance and regulation of the social economy away from borough level. The Centre has been trying to establish a community health centre in a part of Bow which now lies within the boundaries of Newham, but has been hampered by the differing regeneration priorities of the two councils in question. Newham was felt to have a clear vision of its regeneration agenda, which includes stimulating social economy organisations, whereas Tower Hamlets did not. The Centre has also developed close links with Poplar HARCA with which it is helping local residents to create small businesses as part of a supply chain both for the HARCA estates and for firms in Canary Wharf.

Plate 5.4 Canary Wharf from the Barkantine Estate, Isle of Dogs.

What is interesting about the experience of Tower Hamlets is that while all of the projects cited above are 'local' in that they serve the needs of specific areas within the borough, they rely on inputs from activists, networks, and other resources from outside the immediate area. While this has long been the case with some projects – SSBA was started by non-locals in the late 1970s – the practice of external networking seems to be growing. This is in part a consequence of the changing political structure of the capital, which is moving back to a London-wide rather than borough-based or local approach to development. This is reflected in the formation of SEL to represent London's social economy as a whole. It is also the product of the non-localised practices of individual social enterprises. Bromley-by-Bow, for example, which is seen by many as a model of future social enterprise development, does not see itself as a local community project in the strict sense. It is not community-owned, it was set up and is run by professionals from elsewhere and it provides high level, integrated services which could not possibly have been developed using local capacities alone. Indeed, as many of the projects operating in Tower Hamlets have recognised, many of the problems in the borough stem precisely from the isolated and defensive nature of its very varied communities. Success has often come when projects have been able to transcend localness. In some cases, as in that of SSBA and Bromley-by-Bow, this has meant circumventing the existing political structures of the borough, which both see as a hindrance to regeneration and to the exploitation of opportunities that lie elsewhere in London. In that sense the relative absence of the local state in Tower Hamlets from direct involvement in the social economy has prompted the more successful organisations to look beyond local administrative boundaries to find the sort of supportive structures and networks that enable social enterprises to develop and thrive. This raises an important policy question as to whether Third Sector organisations operating in much smaller, and therefore much more limiting, urban environments which lack the economic capacity and diversity and the political variety of London can take advantage of non-local resources in quite the same way.

Conclusion

Although Bristol and Tower Hamlets share some features in common, the nature of the social economy that has developed in each is significantly different. This a product of the differing needs and geographies of the various communities in both, and the resources available there, both in terms of funding and human capabilities. Whereas Bristol has been able to develop an integrated and co-ordinated social economy that has a certain degree of coherence and self-awareness, the Third Sector in Tower Hamlets is more fragmentary and competitive. This is partly a consequence of how the particular social, political, and economic geography of the borough has historically worked against a borough-wide solidarity. Rapid change and the varying geography of funding regimes has also encouraged competitive rather than co-operative approaches. It is also partly a consequence of the access to wider networks in London, in the form of markets, expertise, and resources. This has reduced the need for local cohesion.

But there are also strong similarities of place. In both, successful social enterprises have been able to develop because opportunities exist for committed individuals and groups to develop innovative Third Sector projects. Whereas in economically and socially evacuated cities such as Glasgow and Middlesbrough the local state has taken the lead in the social economy, in Bristol and Tower Hamlets the role of the state has been almost diametrically opposite. The space created by the Third Sector has, perhaps because of this institutional presence, generated a distance on the part of the local state in community-based regeneration. It is, however, the balance between the local state and civic capital that has worked in favour of the social economy.

Moreover, in both Bristol and Tower Hamlets, although in different ways, there is a pool of people with the necessary resources and skills to identify local needs and potential mechanisms for meeting them and the willingness and capacity to get involved in animating activities. Much of the lead has come from faith-based organisations, from environmental groups, and from other activists. But this is not a communitarian leadership, rooted in the energies of the excluded. In both cases, with very few exceptions, those developing and leading Third Sector projects are not members of the local community that they seek to serve, but social entrepreneurs who have made a conscious decision to do so, eschewing the higher salaries and job security of the formal public and private sectors. Crucially, this presupposes the availability of a civic culture and economic capacity which enables them to make such altruistic choices. In Bristol, a long history of alternative and oppositional politics and dissenting religion has created a ready source of people willing to participate in the Third Sector. The prosperity of the city too has generated a certain capacity for the donation of voluntary labour and stints of work in the lower paid social economy. Whereas in Bristol, these conditions exist across the city, with small areas of poverty surrounded by more prosperous communities, in the case of Tower Hamlets projects are having to look beyond the immediate locality. The size of London's economy, society, and polity, including the social economy, has added a huge range of potential contacts, funders, volunteers, and other resources on which a social enterprise can draw. This 'outreach' is also a market for peripatetic social entrepreneurs and professionals, who, as a result, have looser ties than in Bristol within the communities they serve.

Thus, oddly, the success of the social economy in Tower Hamlets and Bristol is a play on a non-local localness. Social enterprise relies to a large extent in breaking down the kinds of intractable localness – born of poverty, racism, discrimination, physical isolation or insularity – which confine poor communities to existing wholly within territorially demarcated local social and institutional structures. It is by going against the grain and challenging the dynamics that create such insular communities, by linking local needs to resources available at other spatial scales and within other economic and political circuits, that the social economy in such places is able to transcend the limitations of place. While place based, they are certainly not place bound. Of course, it helps if those social entrepreneurs are already part of wider networks and if those networks are accessible or proximate. Where such alternatives are not readily available, and where the Third Sector has no choice but to rely on the limited resources of poor people living in poor places, the development of such successful projects is all the more difficult.

Just as social exclusion can be seen to have a distinct geography tied to particular places, so we can conclude that the social 'inclusion' represented by the social economy also has a distinct, though different, geography, one that does not match that of social exclusion. The social economy, despite being routinely linked in policy discourses to poor places, seems to require resources, outlets, and capabilities that typically do not correspond to the geography of social need. They go beyond the local community. Where such access does not exist, the task may well fall to local authorities and local communities, both of which, however, seem ill-equipped to mobilise the social economy in a significant way.

6   Prospects

In this final chapter, we evaluate the prospects of the social economy in light of the evidence gathered. The case histories tell a story of enormous variety within and between places to the point of questioning the very meaning of the term 'the social economy'. At one extreme, some initiatives, though formally non-profit-based, are only marginally different from small private sector enterprises in terms of their business organisation and market practices. Their 'social' commitment lies in facilitating the reinsertion of the socially excluded into the mainstream economy, through support for entrepreneurship (e.g. low-cost premises) or direct employment and schemes to improve employability. At the other extreme, other initiatives are wedded to an alternative economic culture that differs sharply from the market philosophy, centred instead around the provision of socially useful services, meeting needs, ethical trade, and social/community empowerment and democratisation.

The evidence also tells a story of struggle and limited achievement, set against the high policy expectations outlined in the opening chapters which place the social economy at centre stage in the battle against social exclusion. We have come across some wonderful examples of imaginative provision, ethical commitment, and social entrepreneurship. These initiatives should be celebrated. But, they have struggled to get where they are, and they stand out as exceptions in a sector marked by high failure rates, low-quality entrepreneurship, dependence on public sector funding, chronic under-capitalisation, modest job generation, unstable and under-paid employment, and limited community involvement. The powers of the UK social economy taken as whole do not stack up to anywhere close to the policy desiderata we outlined in Chapter 3.

What are the implications of this evidence? We do not wish to claim that the contrast between limited success and widespread failure justifies abandonment of a policy commitment to the social economy. This would do injustice to the achievements of the most successful examples as well as to the very real question of how to meet social needs circumvented by the welfare state and the market. Instead, we wish to use the evidence to sharpen the discussion on what to expect from the social economy, both in terms of realistic goals, and its relationship to the mainstream (state and economy). This discussion is taken up in the second part of the chapter.

In the first part, we identify the factors that seem to have facilitated or hampered the success of social economy. Our aim is not to look for best practice, because our argument is that success and failure are to varying degrees a product of context, and therefore not readily separable or transferable from local and non-local social and institutional settings. The purpose of the discussion, thus, is to shift the policy debate away from a decontextualised, one-fit-for-all approach, towards one that explicitly aligns expectations to contextual variations, local and beyond.

Influences on performance

Given the variety of experience in the social economy, it makes no sense to look for universally-valid factors cutting across varied initiatives, especially given the policy interest today in handbook prescriptions. It is, however, legitimate to ask if there is a recurring set of influences with a decisive impact on performance. Our evidence allows us to identify five factors, with clear implications for what might be considered as the framework conditions for a vibrant social economy.

The first concerns the quality of leadership of the social entrepreneurs and intermediaries. Evidence of the involvement of communities and the socially excluded in establishing initiatives and in driving their success has been most notable by its absence. This is no surprise, given the complex privations of skill, know-how, capability, and confidence which mark the socially excluded. The successful ventures have in general been driven by committed professionals, experienced social entrepreneurs, community activists, and ethical leaders (e.g. in religious or environmental movements). Many are extraordinary individuals who have given up the option of lucrative careers, and who possess a complex array of skills and abilities, to mobilise resources, motivate people, identify under-met needs, make contacts, think laterally, and grasp opportunities. One commentator has described them as 'the research and development wing of the welfare system, innovating new solutions to intractable social problems' (Leadbeater 1997: 8). They are leaders and visionaries, and if not this, at minimum highly professional in their approach to social enterprises as business ventures.

The second, and related, factor is a clarity of goal. Many initiatives that flounder lack a clear sense of mission, and for that fail to align processes with aims. Typically, initiatives mixing business-driven aspirations and cohesion/empower-ment goals, without a conscious understanding of the differences between them, have had to sacrifice one or the other or have come unstuck and fallen between two stools because of contradictory organisational arrangements. For example, ethical ventures have been forced to lower wages or the quality of training because the product is non-viable, or business-driven ventures have been forced by funding agencies to change direction because of poor social achievements. As we noted, this kind of elision played a part in the decline of the community business movement in Scotland. In contrast, the experience of initiatives with clear aims has been differ-ent. Those with cohesion and empowerment as the main goal have consciously organised work, clients and products as a means of meeting needs or developing capabilities, which, in turn, has focused effort. Similarly, business-driven ventures run by professionals, as is the trend now in Glasgow, are clear that equity must follow business success, perhaps even at the expense of social objectives.

Third, there can be no doubt that success is related to systematic and careful market research. The initiatives that have failed or are struggling to survive are those with products and services that are of poor quality, restricted demand, or in competition with other outlets. Only too often they have been borne out of response to a highly localised problem, without analysis of the potential for sustained demand. In contrast, the successful ventures – either ethically or business-driven – offer a unique product, with potential beyond the local economy, and in markets of secondary interest to mainstream private sector firms or public welfare organisations. Typical niches include art materials for child-care organisations, recycled furniture for low-income groups, low-budget catering, shopping catalogues distributed by the homeless, and targeted services for ethnic minorities or particular disadvantaged groups. In all the cases, real under-met social needs have been identified, with potential for expansion out of the immediate neighbourhood as well as into related services. This said, it should be noted that in some instances, the local state has played an important role in underwriting demand as a contractor of the services provided. This highlights that for survival, beyond the important question of choosing the right product, there is a pressing need to secure recurring demand; a considerable challenge for the usually small social enterprise with fragile market expertise and thinly spread competencies.

This brings us to the fourth factor, which relates to the intermediation of risk. The limited resources of social enterprises are typically stretched to the full. Often, as we have seen throughout this book, this is because of their limited business expertise, their relative isolation from circuits of information, services, expertise, and finance, and the lack of involvement on the part of their client-groups and communities who face the worst deprivations of social capital. This insecurity is intensified by the culture of short-termism and bureaucracy that characterises public funding for the sector in the UK. Frequent complaints noted in our study include the absence of medium-term funding, unnecessary paper-work and red-tape, evaluations based primarily on quantified outputs (e.g. number of jobs), intrusive monitoring of performance, partnership with other organisations as a funding requirement, and, more generally, short-termism and frequently changing fashions in urban regeneration policy.

In contrast, the more successful initiatives seem to have benefited from sensitive risk mediation of different kinds. One is funding sensitive to the social targets of the initiatives. This includes recognising the need for balancing social objectives such as empowerment, advocacy, and capacity-building, with quantitative measures of success, recognising the time and resource difficulties posed by an audit-based funding culture, and providing financial latitude for product or process innovation, and, if necessary, failure. Another example is intermediation itself, in the form of conscious effort by enterprises to involve clients and employees, and importantly, the possibility of regular networking among social entrepreneurs and social economy professionals. Finally, within the local state, which continues to play a critical role in funding, enabling, and contracting services to the social economy, an attitude of recognition and partnership, rather than one of prescription or distance, has made a difference.

The fifth factor influencing performance – in many ways an obvious one – is the proximity of initiatives to mainstream economic dynamism. This factor affects both supply and demand conditions. There can be no doubt that social enterprises based in or close to areas of economic prosperity have benefited from better market opportunities linked to a higher and more varied elasticity of demand. There is a greater scope for niche products, sustained by a more varied pattern of consumer expenditure. On the supply side, potentially, the market for funding in prosperous areas is more specialised, affording some room for socially-based investment ventures, while the higher level of churning in the labour market appears to attract, even if only for short periods, a more varied and experienced set of professionals, employees, and clients into the social economy.

How place matters

The evidence that there is a positive correlation between the strength of social enterprises and the local mainstream economy poses an interesting problem for current policy which proposes the social economy as a solution for the economic-ally most marginalised areas. As we saw in Chapter 2, UK government policies (as manifest in the recommendations of the Social Exclusion Unit, new welfare programmes, and neighbourhood regeneration policies) have come to equate the social economy with social exclusion.

This has been achieved through a particularly superficial interpretation of the geographies of the two phenomena and their causes, an elision of the social with the spatial, as we suggested in Chapters 1 and 2. The localised manifestation of social exclusion in its varied forms (e.g. in 'sink' social housing estates and de-industrialised inner-cities) is increasingly read as evidence of the local causes of exclusion (e.g. ghetto cultures, spirals of multiple deprivation, local pathologies of life on the margins). As a corollary, there is a diminishing acknowledgement of wider causes such as the socio-spatial biases of national welfare and competitive-ness policies, the positional weaknesses of particular groups in society (rather than just where they live), and opportunity structures adversely affected by inter-national economic circumstances and intensifying competition in a globalising economy (Chatterton and Bradley 2000; Oatley 2000). This, in turn, has legiti-mated a shift to area-based solutions, including various sorts of community-based schemes incorporating the social economy, on the grounds that social enterprises are supposed to use local resources to respond to local needs. While it is recog-nised that the strength of the social economy varies from place to place, the logic of the new thinking is that a crystallisation of best practice from the experiences of the most successful ventures around the country can help to iron out 'local impediments' and produce generalised and transferable models of 'success'. Local potential can be realised, but only if cleansed of local noise.

Our city case studies, in contrast, have shown that the social economy is the *product* of local noise. It is a creature of social context, and therefore inseparable from it, which is precisely why it is so varied from place to place. This implies that even if it were possible to identify the model social enterprise, its implantation in different places would be difficult, given the powers of context. The important question, however, is what does context mean? We have shown that social context and place are not one and the same, that is, reducible to each other. Instead, our case studies have revealed the centrality of the character of society-in-place (not just society-as-place), with all its varied geographies of local and global connection and being. Put differently, context matters in terms of how the social economy is locally instantiated, rather than as social context reduced to particular types of place (e.g. low- or high-trust environments, spaces of face-to-face familiarity, powers of community, circuits of local need). Places, in our study, have mattered as social formations with varying geographies of connectivity, not as spatial formations.

Indeed, we have seen very few examples of social enterprise rooted in so-called local society defined as community or local social capital, and we have seen few examples of success confined to local circuits of supply, connectivity, and provision. In Glasgow, the most enterprising initiatives have sought national markets, while the new culture of business professionalism in the governance of the sector is not reducible to 'local culture'. Similarly, in both Bristol and Tower Hamlets, opportunities have arisen as a result of peripatetic professionals and mobile standards, together with connections into the wider formal economy. Local commitment and the response to local needs has not depended solely on local resources, nor, ironically, on local society. Here, place has mattered as a site of network connections, while elsewhere, for example in Middlesbrough, where such connections have been largely absent, the local social economy had had no choice but to rely on local links and capabilities. In neither case, however, can the 'local' be seen as pre-given in its character.

In what ways, then, has local context mattered in shaping the social economy? It has done so primarily as an institutional setting with its own peculiar history and character. The discussion in the preceding section on influences on the performance of individual social enterprises should not be detached from this aspect of place. This was amply confirmed in all the city case studies. For example, in the radically hollowed out neighbourhoods, where capabilities on the ground have been tested to the limit by poverty and alienation, the role of the state and top-down support in general, has become crucial. Elsewhere, as we saw in the examples of Bristol and Tower Hamlets, the presence of an active Third Sector, instituted cultural variety, and an ethical middle class, has played a determining role. The 'instanciation' of the social economy – successful or otherwise – has occurred through this institutional context.

Looking across these varied experiences, there are six aspects of local context which appear to have played an important part in influencing the formation of a developed, varied, and relatively independent social economy. They constitute a local cultural environment and support structure for social enterprises to develop without being forced to rely solely on their limited resources and capabilities. In no particular order of importance, these include, first, the presence of voiced minority cultures expressing non-mainstream needs and values. The presence, in different doses and mixes, of outreach artists, environmentalists, New Age groups, yeoman values, women's groups, ethnic minority demands, Quaker, Methodist or other ethical organisations committed to social empowerment, has helped to legitimate and support bottom-up initiatives designed to meet social needs or harness alternative economic values (e.g. fair trade, reciprocity, profit-sharing).

A second aspect, which is in part a consequence of the above, is associational presence, or what Martin Evans (2001) describes as, in the context of the USA and France a market for welfare intermediaries in between the state and the private sector. These intermediaries are not Third Sector organisations plain and simple, but agencies like BACEN in Bristol that have emerged to handle contracted-out state welfare services, and which act as advocates for social enterprises, as a search engine for information, resources, and opportunities, and a contact base within and beyond the sector. The absence of local associations is not only an impediment to mobilisation and interest representation within the social economy, but also skews the balance of power in favour of mainstream organisations that have only a passing or instrumentalist interest in the social economy.

The behaviour of the local state, the third aspect, is a good example of this inter-institutional balance. In contexts of limited local institutional pluralism such as Glasgow and Middlesbrough, the state, with the help of career professionals, has acted as the major player in pursuing a particular model of the social economy, but one in which it can claim no special expertise. This has led to modest outputs, or a predictable alignment of the social economy to small business targets or intermediate labour market goals. In contrast, in settings of greater civic activism and institutional heterogeneity such as Tower Hamlets and Bristol, the local authorities have had to be more imaginative about the possibilities as well as their own role. At times, as Robert Putnam (1993) theorises in the context of regions rich in social capital, this has stimulated an openness to difference and a willingness to support, rather than direct, the effort of social enterprises.

As a consequence, a fourth influence on the social economy relates to the scope for agonism in the local political culture (Mouffe 2000). An agonistic political sphere is one that accepts difference and looks for agreement through vigorous discussion between opposed interests. It does not seek consensus if this means the suppression of plural and minority interests, but looks for a commons constructed out of debate and disagreement, a democracy based on the right of presence of diverse interests. Such a political culture – in part evident in Bristol – can be vital for the social economy for two reasons. First, because it gives space to what is normally considered a minority economic activity. Second, because it accepts the legitimacy of economic (as well as social and political) experimentation and novelty. Related to this openness is a readiness to avoid a politics of place based around an inward-looking local sense of place (e.g. a culture of 'we have always done it this way', or 'our field of engagement ends at the city boundary'). Instead, we see a politics *in* place that is not reducible to a local sense *of* place, one that draws on a wider field of connections, resources, and ideas to vitalise the social economy in imaginative ways, among other things.

Thus, a fifth aspect of place that is of significance is connectivity. Localities such as Bristol and Tower Hamlets with more than just a handful of successful social enterprises are places of socio-economic mobility and external linkage. This is manifest in different ways including the to-and-fro between work and employment, informal meetings between social entrepreneurs and activists, the presence of peripatetic professionals, strong 'movement' links beyond the locality, juxtaposition with the formal economy, and linkage between communities, local authorities, and intermediaries. These localities are like network sites, able to reach out to sustain the social economy, while localised clusters of activity such as Glasgow and Middlesbrough lack lateral connectivity or are characterised by connections established and/or appropriated by the state.

Finally, however, underpinning all of the above, is the extent of local socio-economic deprivation. There can be little doubt that the differences observed between the four cities examined here are linked to the depth and scale of deprivation. Places with large-scale and structural unemployment in a context of limited labour market vitality, evacuation of civil society, and reduced social heterogeneity, possess a restricted resource and opportunity base for social enterprise. The excluded are least equipped to participate and the institutional base to facilitate integration is deficient. The situation, as we have seen, is very different in places of relative prosperity, labour market churning, and socio-cultural heterogeneity, where the opportunity field is broader as is the base for sustaining economic variety.

The above six aspects of place overlap with the influences on individual performance that we identified earlier. The key point, however, is that the characteristics of place are not reducible local attributes, but in contributing to the culture of a place, they ensure that the social economy remains varied and unique in different locations. In this sense, current policy sensitivity to local efforts in combating social exclusion is correct. However, this sensitivity, we have suggested, is not produced from an awareness of the powers and constraints of context, but a stereotyping of the places that suffer social exclusion, and of the requisite (social economy) solutions. In addition, the policy focus is primarily on individual-level interventions, not on the collective and at times intangible place aspects that we have identified. Yet, any committed attempt to build the social economy needs to take these aspects seriously.

What kind of social economy and for whom?

The fundamental normative question, however, is what do we want the social economy for? In the current excitement, at least three positions are evident, linked, respectively, to state welfare reform, business enterprise, and the economy of needs.

Regarding the first position, as we suggested in Chapter 1, much contemporary policy interest in the social economy, not just in the UK, is driven by concerns to reform the welfare state. Social enterprises have been welcomed as labour market intermediaries, facilitating the re-entry of the socially excluded into employment, because they are seen as resource-efficient and close to 'communities'. They are also seen to help the contracting out of services traditionally offered by the welfare state, thereby reducing the cost of welfare provision and normalising a new culture of welfare pluralism. There is an odd consensus emerging between Third Way politicians interested in efficiency of delivery and reduced state expenditure/ dependency, and social economy advocates thrilled by the prospect of becoming co-producers of welfare services and 'putting the public back into public service'.[1] Finally, the social economy – through its varied local powers ranging from the offer of work and services to empowerment and community/capability-building – is seen as a bottom-up way of combating social exclusion, now pathologised as the problem of particular types of people in particular types of location. Much of all this can be read as a subtle abandonment of the universal welfare state under the guise of partnership, efficiency of service delivery, and local targeting.

We have no quarrel with the idea that the Third Sector, and specifically social enterprises, have an important role to play in welfare provision through their expertise and commitment. We are not convinced, however, that this should amount to state welfare *substitution*. Our study tells a story of patchy and limited success in the social economy, hampered in many instances by poor funding, stretched resources, erratic and modest quality services, and limited survival prospects. It also tells the story of social enterprises simply plastering over the cracks of composite welfare deprivation in places of long-term decline, unable to cover the demand, sustain provision, and, most importantly, rebuild capabilities. In this context, it is not hard to conclude that the social economy could become, full circle back into the nineteenth century, a poor form of welfare for the poor, as the welfare state realigns to reproduce those most economically useful.

The risk is of ending one-nation politics and one-nation welfare society, in preference of a hot-spot geography of exclusion and inclusion that rarely finds its sources within the named places. To avoid this prospect requires continuation of a welfare culture of complementary support through a social economy funded properly by the state within a framework, as in the Scandinavian countries, of active state measures offering work opportunities to the excluded and welfare schemes of high quality designed to build the capabilities of all, not the few.

The second normative expectation from the social economy relates to the ethos of enterprise and business ingrained by neoliberalism in virtually every aspect of social life. This emphasis has grown within the sector itself, often as a means of selling social enterprises to government and other sponsors, but also, as we have seen in this study, as a means of legitimating social enterprise as a market-driven, revenue-seeking venture. There is growing unease with labels such as 'not-for-profit', 'community business', or 'needs before profit'. This shift has occurred as a result of the perception as we saw in the case of Scotland that old-style community initiatives were not run as proper businesses (by poor product viability, no business expertise, lack of organisation, etc.) and therefore failed to survive or grow. The shift is also related to a new sense that commercial and social objectives can and must be reconciled, otherwise the reputation of social enterprises will remain that of 'small, undercapitalised, commercially precarious enterprises providing a limited number of poorly-paid, low-skilled jobs that are funded as an arm of social policy' (Hayton 2000: 205). For Keith Hayton:

> If community business is to make a significant contribution then there is a need to adopt a more targeted development approach which could result in the setting up of a number of exemplar businesses that are commercially viable and are involved in mainstream competitive markets.
>
> (2000: 204)

Hayton goes on to recommend reforms to improve the business development skills of social entrepreneurs, recruit board members from the private sector, target support across the life of a business, and focus on targets such as increases in turnover and trading surpluses.

While we endorse the view that social enterprises should not become sites of economic misery or poor professional practice, we are sceptical about how far they can be seen as just another (mainstream) market venture. What makes them distinct from commercial firms is their commitment to social empowerment and meeting social needs. Commercial firms are successful as businesses in part because of the absence of such a commitment, which allows them to maximise profit and revenue to shareholders. Jobs and job satisfaction are a by-product, not the prime goal. Conversely, one reason why social enterprises fail as businesses is that their prime social obligations – which require care, spending time with clients, investing resources in people, involvement in the community – might conflict with the requirement of market efficiency and market-driven product viability. In short, failure may be a consequence of being forced to become commercial businesses in ways which compromise their original social objectives. Our study has shown that when ventures have not been evaluated by sponsors on strict commercial criteria, and when there is a degree of financial security provided by funding agencies, the scope to develop as enterprises with a social remit has been considerably enhanced.

Our study has also shown that few social enterprises have managed to develop niche products with sustainable or growing demand, and that when they have, public sector support has not been far away. This raises the question of whether it is realistic to assume that the majority of social enterprises can become commercial enterprises, even with the kind of support Hayton recommends. The restricted commercial capabilities of the communities in which they are based, their severe resource, know-how, and size constraints, and the inelasticity of demand in their immediate local market, place them at the very jagged end of business viability. They are constrained by local circumstances and they lack the resources to connect into wider networks. In this context, talk of commercial viability and business potential seems somewhat wishful and potentially a distraction from the main purpose of social enterprises. A more sensible alternative, especially in areas of marked deprivation and isolation from economic opportunity, might be the renewal of effort by the state to increase job opportunities through incentives to the private sector or through public sector programmes, instead of passing responsibility on to the social economy.

It is the alterity of the social economy from the mainstream, rooted in the economy of social needs, that offers the greatest potential for the future. In the market society accompanied by waning state provision, the culture of economic organisation for competitiveness and consumerism is marginalising the idea of economic organisation for meeting social needs, fostering social solidarity, and developing human capabilities. Marx famously described this contrast as the opposition between production for exchange-value and production for use-value. Today, the dislocation is leaving vast sections of society without adequate welfare provision, under-met needs, a limited role as producers in the context of jobless growth, and alienation from full citizenship through entrapment in ghettos of social exclusion. And, the twist is that the pervasive reach of exchange-value society makes it increasingly difficult to imagine and legitimate non-market forms of organisation and provision. The elision between ethics, needs, and market performance in expectations from the social enterprise of the future is symptomatic of this turn.

Yet in our study what has marked the success and energy of enterprises such as the Arts Factory, Gabalfa, Matson, SOFA, FRC, Account 3, the Bridge Project, and the Bromley-by-Bow Centre is the legitimacy they give to the possibility of a different kind of economy. They are driven by an ethical commitment to social empowerment and to the welfare/developmental needs of marginalised groups, and it is through this commitment that they have fashioned products and services. They see what they do as advocacy for another way of life; one based on social commitment, ethical/environmental citizenship, and work as a vehicle for self and social enhancement. They have a clear sense of why they merit the label *social* enterprise, and they are part of a wider social desire for an alternative to market society.

This seems to be the real strength of the social economy. It can never become a growth machine or an engine of job generation, or a substitute for the welfare state, but it can stand as a small symbol of another kind of economy, one based on meeting social needs and enhancing social citizenship. For this, the characterisation of the social economy as a 'localised' solution to the problem of 'local' social exclusion must be broken. Such a characterisation of the social economy rules out speculation of systemic alternatives to the mainstream economy. The key move is to 'de-localise' discourses around the social economy and to challenge the dominant conception of the mainstream, rather than to cast the social economy in the image of the mainstream and in the interstices that the mainstream has abandoned.

Appendix: the sample projects

Project title	Location
460 Community Training and Resource Project	London
Aashyana Housing Association	SW England
Access North Ayr	Scotland
Accident Prevention Loan Scheme	London
Account 3	London
Action in the Community for Employment (ACE)	NW England
ADAPT NI	N Ireland
ADEPT Community Development Agency	NW England
Adult Basic Skills Resource Centre	N Ireland
Al-Hasaniya Moroccan Women's Project	London
Amble Development Trust	NE England
Amman Valley Enterprises	Wales
Antrim People First	N Ireland
Aquila Housing Association	NE England
Arena Art and Design Association	Merseyside
Armagh Confederation of Voluntary Groups	N Ireland
Association of Greater London Older Women	London
Association of Independent Advice Centres	N Ireland
Ballycastle Cross Community Choral Society	N Ireland
Ballyoran Centre Ballybeen Ltd	N Ireland
Barnoldswick Disability Project	NW England
Bedford Community Arts	E England
Beechmount Community Project	N Ireland
Belfast Womens Training Services	N Ireland
Blaenllechau Community Regeneration	Wales
Bridge Project	London
Bristol Area Community Enterprise Network	SW England
Broadstone Aid	SW England
Brokenborough and District Community Development Association	N Ireland

Project title	Location
Bromley-by-Bow Centre	London
Brouhaha International	Merseyside
Building Blocks	London
Calton Child Care	Scotland
Castlemilk Electronic Village	Scotland
Centre for Employment and Enterprise Development	SW England
Chinese Mental Health Association	London
Citizen Advocacy	E England
Coin Street Community Builders	London
Combiz	NE England
Community Action Regeneration Project	SW England
Community Campus (Cleveland) Ltd	NE England
Community Enterprise in Strathclyde	Scotland
Community Inclusion for Deaf and Hard of Hearing People	N Ireland
Community Self-Build Agency	NE England
Community Self-Build Scotland	Scotland
Community Volunteer Training in Playwork	N Ireland
Community Work Training and Apprenticeship Project	N Ireland
Conradh na Gaeilge	N Ireland
Coventry and Warwickshire Community Safety	Midlands
Craigmillar Festival Society	Scotland
Cumbernauld YMCA–YWCA Foyer Project	Scotland
Derry Travellers Support Group	N Ireland
Derry Well Woman	N Ireland
Design Options for a Versatile Environment	SW England
Dove Designs	Merseyside
Down Visually Impaired Persons	N Ireland
Durham Co-operative Development Association	NE England
East Antrim Community Development Service Ltd	N Ireland
East End Partnership	Scotland
Easton Business Centre	SW England
Environmental Youth Work	London
Estate Action Areas	Merseyside
Ex-Offender Guidance/Basic Skills Programme	E England
Family Caring Centre	N Ireland
Fermanagh Community Care Training	N Ireland
Finsbury Park Action group	London
Foleshill Area Coordination	Midlands
Food Provision Programme	SW England
Forth Spring	N Ireland
Free Form Arts Trust	London
Furniture Resource Centre	Merseyside
Future Ways	N Ireland

Project title	Location
Gabalfa Community Workshop	Wales
George House Trust	NW England
Glasgow Alliance	Scotland
Glasgow Works	Scotland
Govan Workspace Ltd	Scotland
Greencastle Women's Group	N Ireland
Greenwich Co-operative Development Agency	London
Greysteel Community Enterprises	N Ireland
Grove Hill 2000	NE England
Group Organisation and Leadership	N Ireland
Gutteridge Wood Management Project	London
Hartcliffe and Withywood Ventures	SW England
Havering Council for Voluntary Service	SW England
Heeley City Farm	NW England
Helping Hands	N Ireland
Hereford and Worcestershire Credit Union Development Agency	Midlands
Irish in Greenwich Project	London
Keady and District Development Community Initiative	N Ireland
Konteka Bus Project	Merseyside
Ladywood Fast Track	Midlands
Langridge Initiative Centre	NE England
Latymer Training	London
Leathermarket Joint Management Board	London
Little Venice Housing Co-operative	London
Local Labour in Construction	London
Local People Local Voice	NW England
Loftus Development Trust	NE England
London Connection Workspace Project	London
Luton Foyer	E England
Magnet Young Adult Centre	N Ireland
Making Music Work	NE England
Manchester People First	NW England
Manufacturing and Prosperity in the Coalfields	NE England
Matson Neighbourhood Project	SW England
Merseyside Trade Union, Community and Unemployed Resource Centre	Merseyside
Monagh Developments	N Ireland
Moor Nook Estate Management Board/Food Co-operative	NW England
Morton Community Centre	N Ireland
Mosscare Housing Association	NW England
New Barracks TMC	NW England
Newham City Farm	London
NICOD Training Services	N Ireland

Project title	Location
Northern Ireland Community Addiction Service	N Ireland
Off the Streets, Into Work	London
Older Homeless Peoples' Project	NW England
Ollerton and District Economic Forum	Midlands
One Plus	Scotland
Opportunity Youth	N Ireland
Paisley Partnership	Scotland
Pathway Employment Service	London
Pathway Outdoor Adventure	Midlands
Pathways	Scotland
Peat Rigg	NE England
Pecan Ltd	London
Penarth Family and Community Resource Centre	Wales
Penygraig Community Project	Wales
Penywaun Enterprise Partnership	Wales
Pimlico Village Housing Co-op	London
Planning Aid for London	London
Poplar HARCA	London
Portsmouth Foyer	SW England
Princes Trust Volunteers Programme	E England
Project Denton	London
Project Ty Cynon	Wales
Reach for Success	NE England
Reading YMCA Foyer	E England
Reclaim	NW England
Retford Action Centre	Midlands
Richmond Park Horticultural Project	E England
Ropen Street Community Development Group	N Ireland
Rostrevor Women's Group	N Ireland
Rotherham Credit Union Development	NW England
Sense of Sound Workshops	Merseyside
Shankill Women's Centre	N Ireland
Sheltered Help	N Ireland
Skill Development	N Ireland
Social Development Project	E England
Social Integration and Vocational/Social Skills Development for Adolescents	London
SOFA	SW England
South Bristol Community Builders	SW England
South Bristol Learning Network	SW England
South Tyneside Arts Studio	NE England
South Tyneside Training and Enterprise Network	NE England
Spitalfields Small Business Association	London

Project title	Location
Springfield Horseshoe Housing Co-op	Midlands
St Hilda's Partnership	NE England
St Martin-in-the-Fields Social Care Unit	London
St Matthew's Special Needs Group	N Ireland
St Peter's Urban Village Trust	Midlands
Steps into Employment	London
Swan Foyer	E England
The Arts Factory	Wales
The Cedar Centre	London
The Childrens Scrapstore	SW England
The Duffryn Project	Wales
The Factory Community Centre	London
The Gorbals Initiative	Scotland
The Local Initiative Team	NE England
The New and Old Gurnos and Galon Uchaf Regeneration Project	Wales
The Pulse	N Ireland
The VIVA Project	Wales
The Wise Group	Scotland
Third Wave	Midlands
Tower Hamlets Co-operative Development Agency	London
Tower Hamlets Health Strategy Group	London
Townsend Street Social Outreach Centre	N Ireland
Upper Andersonstown Community Forum	N Ireland
Urban Challenge	E England
Urban Oasis	NW England
UTOPIA Project	N Ireland
Voluntary Action Lochaber	Scotland
Voluntary Hostels Group Resettlement Scheme	E England
Wales and West Housing Association	Wales
Watford and District YMCA Foyer	E England
Wester Hailes Partnership	Scotland
Wheelchair Basketball in Northern Ireland	N Ireland
Women Into Politics	N Ireland
Women Mean Business: Film, Video and Drama Association	London
Working for Childcare	London
Working with Villages	SW England
Wrekin Homecare Co-operative	Midlands
Youth Focus	London
Ystalyfera Development Trust	Wales

Notes

Preface

1 The complete database went on-line in early 2001 and can be viewed at http://locin.jrc.it

1 The social economy in context

1 See for example: 'The Emergence of Social Enterprises in Europe': http://www.emes.net
2 See 3rd system: Four Models for Four Realities: http://www.fondazionecesar.it

2 Social economy, social exclusion, localisation

1 For example, EUROSTAT data reveal spatial concentrations of poor housing, unemployment and ill health throughout the EU (for example, see Commission of the European Communities 1996).
2 It is important to note, however, that there is no necessary reason as to why such organisations automatically have these attributes. There is evidence that often they reproduce rather than challenge inequalities integral to the formal economy (see Bowring 1998). For example, Borzaga and Maiello (1998: 33) recognise that 'social enterprises are characterized by wages lower than those paid by public production units' but go on to assert that this is 'off-set by other aspects of the work'. Borzaga (n.d.: 15–16) argues that these lower wages, plus 'high flexibility in the use of their workforces' are central to the way in which social enterprises can 'curb costs' and in this way match the efficiency of 'for-profit firms'. This comes dangerously close to advocating super-exploitation as the basis of competing with mainstream enterprises.
3 Such views are by no means confined to the European Commission and are widely held in a variety of national Governments and international organisations. For example, in a speech to the World Bank's annual meeting in Hong Kong in 1997, its President proposed that 'meeting the challenge of social inclusion' should be the Bank's main priority:

> our goal must be to reduce these disparities across and within countries, to bring more people into the economic mainstream, to promote equitable access to the benefits of development regardless of nationality, race, or gender. This . . . Challenge of Inclusion . . . is the key development challenge of our time.
>
> (Wolfensohn 1997)

In the same year, the Director General of the International Labour Organization discussed the connection between exclusion and unemployment:

> These phenomena [of social exclusion] are very often a reflection of exclusion from the world of work (long-term unemployment, termination of unemployment

benefits, poor level of training of young people, and single women, etc.) or precarious employment on the labour market (involuntary part-time work, fixed-term employment, 'odd-jobbing').

(Hansenne, 1997)

While he concedes that those in employment might also be subject to the many pressures that can contribute to exclusion, the emphasis is almost wholly towards unemployment as the cause and reemployment as the solution to social exclusion.

4   In a series of publications the European Commission (CEC 1996, 1998a,b) has compiled a list of nineteen areas of economic activity that it considers capable of generating 'tailor-made jobs' and laying the basis for creating local social economies across Europe (and by implication, more widely). These are: home-help services, childminding, new information and communication technologies, the improvement of the built environment, public and domestic safety, local public transport, the improvement of urban public areas, local shops, energy conservation, tourism, audio-visual, economic development of cultural assets, local cultural development, sport, waste management, water management, protection of rural areas, environmental regulation, and control of pollution.

5   Speech by the Secretary of State for Social Security and Minister for Women, Harriet Harman MP, at the launch of the Centre for the Analysis of Social Exclusion, London School of Economics, 13 November 1997. Mimeo. p. 10.

6   From April 2001 New Deal was extended to people aged over 25 who had been out of work for more than 18 months.

7   PATs were established under the remit of government ministers in ten different Whitehall Departments covering: 1 – Jobs, 2 – Skills, 3 – Business, 4 – Neighbourhood management, 5 – Housing management, 6 – Neighbourhood wardens, 7 – Unpopular housing, 8 – Anti-social behaviour, 9 – Community self-help, 10 – Arts and sport, 11 – 'Schools Plus', 12 – Young people, 13 – Shops, 14 – Financial services, 15 – Information technology, 16 – Learning lessons, 17 – Joining it up locally, and 18 – Better information.

8   The report was published to meet the SEU's remit to report to Prime Minister Blair on how to, 'develop integrated and sustainable approaches to the problems of the worst housing estates, including crime, drugs, unemployment, community breakdown, and bad schools, etc.' (SEU 1998: iv).

9   The remit of the SEU only covers England, with responsibility for related programmes in Scotland, Wales, and Northern Ireland falling to the respective government offices and/or the devolved assemblies created in the summer of 1999. Parallel schemes have been put in place in Scotland and Wales. Locations of the thirty-nine current NDC projects can be found through the DETR website at http://www.regeneration. detr.gov.uk/ndc/overview/index.htm (11 May 2001).

10 It is worth recalling Conservative Prime Minister Harold MacMillan's oft-misquoted speech at a garden party in Bedford in 1957: 'Let us be frank about it. *Most* of our people have never had it so good' [emphasis added].

3   Policy and practice in the UK social economy

1   In addition to this primary and original research, we also draw selectively upon cases reported elsewhere in the literature, as well as other research by Ray Hudson, Huw Beynon, and Katy Bennett funded by the Joseph Rowntree Foundation (see Bennett *et al*. 2000).

2   Note 4, Chapter 2 provides a full listing of these fields.

3   Although the César Foundation estimates that 2–3 per cent of national employment in Europe is in the social economy: see Chapter 2.

4   Interview, September 2000.

5 These partnerships are discussed more fully in the next chapter in the context of the social economy in Glasgow.

4 The corporatist social economy: Glasgow and Middlesbrough

1 Indeed early in 2001 a series of closures and redundancy announcements emphasised the extent to which they remain a vulnerable branch plant economy, still susceptible to external control and dependency (cf. Firn 1975).
2 For the purpose of comparability, these graphs are shown on the same scale as those for Bristol and Tower Hamlets in Figure 5.1 on page 85.
3 The map for Middlesbrough (p. 57) is based on the DLTR's (1998) Index of Multiple Deprivation figures which employ a range of employment and lifestyle indicators to develop a ranking of English wards according to their relative deprivation. The ranking runs from 1 (most deprived) to 8414 (least deprived). The map of Glasgow (p. 55) is based on the Scottish Executive's (2000) figures for multiple deprivation in the 894 Scottish postcode districts (PDCs). The figures use a similar range of indicators to produce a ranking for PDCs in Scotland which ranges from 1 (most deprived) to 894 (least deprived).
4 Defined by the DETR as follows:

> Local Concentration is the population weighted average of the ranks of a district's most deprived wards that contain exactly 10 per cent of the district's population. Local Concentration (formerly 'Intensity') is an important way of identifying districts' 'hot spots' of deprivation. The Local Concentration measure defines the 'hot spots' by reference to a percentage of the district's population.
>
> (DTLR 2000)

5 GEAR was one of the early high-profile projects of the Scottish Development Agency, following its establishment in 1975.
6 Scottish Enterprise Glasgow is the relaunched (2001) Glasgow Development Agency (GDA). While the GDA placed considerable emphasis on Third Sector development in all of its policy literature, the relaunched agency has noticeably shifted emphasis much more towards attracting and developing private sector activities and inward investment. The effects of this shift in emphasis on regeneration policy in the city remain to be seen.
7 The seven LDCs are: the Castlemilk Economic Development Agency, the Gorbals Initiative, the Govan Initiative, the Greater Easterhouse Development Company, Drumchapel Opportunities, the East End Partnership, and Glasgow North Ltd.
8 The only other of the original Community Businesses to have survived in Glasgow is Possil Community Business Ltd.
9 The ILM model was one element used by the Labour government in the design of the Welfare-to-Work scheme (see Chapter 2). Although Wise acted as consultants to the policy design process, and despite close links between the Chief Executive and the Prime Minister's office, Wise has been highly critical of Welfare-to-Work, particularly with regard to the compulsory nature of the programme and because it only provides training for a maximum of six months.
10 The study examined attitudes of residents on two estates in Teesside; St Hilda's in Middlesbrough and Norton Grange in Stockton-on-Tees.
11 Although beyond the remit of our study, there is also the substantial A19 Credit Union, one of the largest in the UK, which operates throughout the former county of Cleveland.
12 Interview, Middlesbrough Council 13 October 1999
13 The same is true of the Tayside model on which Combiz was based which has failed to produce any sustainable community enterprise, but has created a small private sector company (Hayton 2000).

5 The distributed social economy: Bristol and Tower Hamlets

1 Interview, Hartcliffe and Withywood Ventures.
2 The maps for Bristol (p. 89) and Tower Hamlets (p. 90) are based on the DLTR's (1998) Index of Multiple Deprivation figures which employ a range of employment and lifestyle indicators to develop a ranking of English wards according to their relative deprivation. The ranking runs from 1 (most deprived) to 8414 (least deprived).
3 For example, the Artangel Trust's 'Inner City' project which worked with a number of artists and writers at the Whitechapel Gallery to produce images and words about the nature of the inner city and which included Augusto Boal who pioneered the use of drama and the arts as a tool of community political empowerment in Brazil and other parts of Latin America. See: http://www.innercity.demon.co.uk/index.htm
4 For further details see: http://www.whitechapel.org.uk/
5 Interview, Easton Workspace.
6 Quakerism took root in Bristol during the mid-seventeenth century. The world's first Methodist Chapel, John Wesley's 'New Room', was founded in Bristol in 1739 and ever since the city has been an important centre for Methodist training and practice.
7 For details see: http://ourworld.compuserve.com/homepages/bgp/
8 Full details of the first twenty-five years of Bristol FoE's activities can be found at http://www.joolz.demon.co.uk/infoe/oct96/happybday.html
9 Interview, leader Tower Hamlets Council, 13 January 2000.
10 Interview, Helena Taggart, Bristol Area Community Enterprise Network.
11 http://www.triodos.co.uk/
12 The name is derived from the acronym for Shifting Old Furniture About. Although there are many similarities between SOFA and the Furniture Resource Centre described in Chapter 3, there are no formal links between the projects.
13 Of approximately 2000 projects of all kinds considered during the course of our research into the social economy, Scrapstore is the only operational workers' collective that we have encountered.
14 Interview, Ray Sefia, CEED, 9 July 1999.
15 Anecdotally, while waiting for an interview with one social enterprise and pondering the reason for Bristol's particular success in developing Third Sector enterprises, one of the researchers drew attention to the copy of the Bristol Yellow Pages which was being used to prop open the door of the office. It was fully three inches thick and seemed to provide in itself a significant part of the explanation.
16 Interview, Helena Taggart, 1999.
17 This contrasts strongly with the positive perception of the Castlemilk project held within Glasgow: see Chapter 4, pp. 67–8.
18 The authors would like to express their gratitude to the London Borough of Tower Hamlets (LBTH) council for their permission to reproduce this map. In doing so the council asked us to point out that it is making considerable efforts to counter the uneven distribution of regeneration activities in the Borough and, through a recently established voluntary sector network is beginning to overcome the limitations of this fragmentary picture. It should also be noted that such fragmented geographies of regeneration availability are by no means confined to Tower Hamlets, but are characteristic of most large conurbations in the UK.
19 St Margaret's House provides subsidised office space for voluntary and Third Sector organizations, often for short periods of time while they find their own premises or for the duration of fixed term projects.
20 Similar campaigns have been mounted in other UK cities, most notably Glasgow and Birmingham, where similar attempts to transfer housing stock to Third or private sector housing associations are under way.
21 Bromley-by-Bow has rapidly become very well known as a model social enterprise,

being cited by the SEU as an example of best practice and being visited by, among others, the Prime Minister.

6 Prospects

1 To borrow a phrase from Ed Mayo of the New Economics Foundation, in a presentation to a conference launching The UK Social Economy Coalition, 31 May 2001, London.

Bibliography

Alcock, P., Gamble, A., Gough, I., Lee, P. and Walker, A. (eds) (1989) *The Social Economy and the Democratic State: A New Policy Agenda for the 1990s*. London, Lawrence and Wishart.

Altvater, E. (1993) *The Future of the Market: An Essay on the Regulation of Money and Nature after the Collapse of Actually Existing Socialism*. London, Verso.

Amin, A., Cameron, A. and Hudson, R. (1999) 'Welfare as Work? The Potential of the UK Social Economy', *Environment and Planning A*, 31, 11:2033–51.

Anheier, H. K. and Seibel, W. (eds) (1990) *The Third Sector: Comparative Studies of Nonprofit Organizations*. Berlin/New York, Walter de Gruyter.

Bassett, K. (1996) 'Partnerships, Business Elites and Urban Politics: New Forms of Partnership in an English City', *Urban Studies* 33, 3: 539–55.

Bauman, Z. (1998) *Work, Consumerism and the New Poor*. Buckingham, Open University Press.

Beck, U., Giddens, A. and Lash, S. (1994) *Reflexive Modernization: Politics, Tradition and Aesthetics in the Modern Social Order*. Cambridge, Polity Press.

Bennett, K., Beynon, H. and Hudson, R. (2000) *Coalfields Regeneration: Dealing with the Consequences of Industrial Decline*. Bristol, Policy Press.

Beynon, H., Hudson, R. and Sadler, D. (1994) *A Place Called Teesside: Locality in a Global Economy*. Edinburgh, Edinburgh University Press.

Birkholzer, K. (1996) 'Social Economy, Community Economy and Third Sector: Fashionable Slogans or Building Blocks for the Future?', *Bauhaus Dessau Foundation, People's Economy: Approaches Towards a New Social Europe*, 41–4.

Blair, T. (1997a) *The Third Way: New Politics for the New Century* (Fabian Pamphlet 588). London, The Fabian Society.

—— (1997b) 'The Will to Win', Speech delivered by UK Prime Minister Tony Blair on Monday 2 June at the Aylesbury Estate, Southwark. Mimeo. Available from: http://www.cabinet-office.gov.uk/seu/index/more.html

—— (2001) 'Speech delivered by UK Prime Minister at the launch of the Neighbourhood Renewal Strategy'. London, 15 January. Mimeo.

Boddy, M., Lovering, J. and Bassett, K. (1986) *Sunbelt City? A Study of Economic Change in Britain's M4 Growth Corridor*. London, Routledge.

Borzaga, C. (n.d.) *The EMES Network: The Emergence of Social Enterprises in Europe*. Trento, Institute for Development Studies of Non-profit Enterprises, 18 pages.

Borzaga, C. and Maiello, M. (1997) 'The Contribution of the Social Enterprise to the Creation of New Employment: The Field of Personal Services'. University of Trento/ Consorzio G. Mattarelli. Unpublished paper. Mimeo.

—— (1998) 'The Development of Social Enterprises' in C. Borzaga and A. Santuari (eds)

Social Enterprises and New Employment in Europe. Trento, Regione Autonoma Trentino-Alto Adige/European Commission DG5: 73–92.

Bowring, F. (1998) 'LETS: An Eco-Socialist Initiative?', *New Left Review*, No. 232, November–December: 91–111.

Bucek, J. and Smith, B. (2000) 'New Approaches to Local Democracy: Direct Democracy, Participation and the "Third Sector"', *Environment and Planning C*, 18: 3–16.

Byrne, D. (1999) *Social Exclusion*. Buckingham, Open University Press.

Carmichael, P. and Midwinter, A. (1999) 'Glasgow: Anatomy of a Fiscal Crisis', *Local Government Studies*, 25, 1 (Spring): 84–98.

Cassell, G. (1923) *The Theory of Social Economy*. London, T. Fisher Unwin.

Catterall, B., Lipietz, A., Hutton, W. and Girardet, H. (1996) 'The Third Sector, Urban Regeneration and the Stakeholder', *City*, No. 5–6: 86–97.

Chatterton, P. and Bradley, D. (2000) 'Bringing Britain Together? The Limitations of Area-based Regeneration Policies in Addressing Deprivation', *Local Economy*, 15, 2: 98–111.

City of Edinburgh Council (1999) 'Management Review of Craigmillar Projects: Progress Report', *Report of the Policy and Resources Committee Urban Regeneration Sub-Committee*, 15 June. Available from City of Edinburgh Council.

Clarke, S. E. (1993) 'The New Localism: Local Politics in a Global Era', in E. G. Goetz and S. E. Clarke (eds) *The New Localism: Comparative Urban Politics in a Global Era*. Newbury Park, CA, Sage: 1–21.

Commission of the European Communities (CEC) (1994) *Growth, Competitiveness, Employment: The Challenges and Ways Forward into the 21st Century*. White Paper. Luxembourg, Office for Official Publications of the European Communities (OOPEC).

—— (1996) *First Report on Economic and Social Cohesion*. Luxembourg, OOPEC.

—— (1998a) *The Era of Tailor-Made Jobs: Second Report on Local Development and Employment Initiatives*. SEC 98, 25 – January, Brussels, European Commission.

—— (1998b) *The Third System and Employment: A First Reflection*. Brussels, European Commission D5/A4 and the European Parliament.

Community Development Project Inter-Project Editorial Team (1977) *Gilding the Ghetto: The State and the Poverty Experiments*. London, Community Development Project (CDP).

Confalonieri, M. A. and Newton, K. (1995) 'Taxing and Spending: Tax Revolt or Tax Protest?', in O. Borre and E. Scarbrough (eds) *The Scope of Government*. Oxford, Oxford University Press: 121–48.

Danson, M. and Mooney, G. (1998) 'Glasgow: A Tale of Two Cities? Disadvantage and Exclusion on the European Periphery', in P. Lawless, R. Martin and S. Hardy (eds) *Unemployment and Social Exclusion: Landscapes of Labour Inequality*. London and Philadelphia, PA, Regional Studies Association/Jessica Kingsley.

Davis, E. (1999) 'The Way Through the Welfare Wood', in A. Kilmarnock (ed.) *The Social Market and the State*. London, Social Market Foundation.

de Leonardis, O. (1998) *In un Diverso Welfare*. Milan, Feltrinelli.

Department of the Environment Transport and the Regions (DETR) (1998) *New Deal for Communities*. London, DETR.

Department of Social Security (DSS) (1998a) *New Ambitions for our Country: A New Contract for Welfare*. London, DSS (cm 3805).

Department of Transport, Local Government and the Regions (DTLR) (2000) *Index of Multiple Deprivation 2000*. London, DTLR. Available from: Index of Multiple Deprivation 2000, DTLR: http://www.regeneration.dtlr.gov.uk/research/id2000/index.htm

Dickson, N. (1997) 'Welfare to Where?', *New Statesman*, 1 August: 18–20.

Donnison, D. (1994) *Act Local: Social Justice from the Bottom Up*. London, IPPR, Commission on Social Justice.

DTZ Pieda Consulting (1999) *Review of Management, Structure and Role of Organisations and Projects in Craigmillar: Final Report*. Edinburgh, City of Edinburgh Council, 9 March.

Dunford, M. and Hudson, R. (1996) *Successful European Regions: Northern Ireland Learning from Others*, Research Monograph No. 3. Belfast, Northern Ireland Economic Council.

Eade, J. (ed.) (1997) *Living in the Global City: Globalization as a Local Process*. London, Routledge.

Ekins, P. (ed.) (1986) *The Living Economy: A New Economics in the Making*. London, Routledge and Kegan Paul.

—— (1992) *A New World Order: Grassroots Movements for Global Change*. London, Routledge.

Ekins, P. and Newby, L. (1998) 'Sustainable Wealth Creation at the Local Level in an Age of Globalisation', *Regional Studies: Journal of the Regional Studies Association*, 32, 9: 863–71.

Esping-Andersen, G. (ed.) (1996) *Welfare States in Transition: National Adaptations in Global Economies*. London, Sage.

Etzioni, A. (1973) 'The Third Sector and Domestic Missions', *Public Administration Review*, 33: 314–23.

—— (1995) *The Spirit of Community: Rights, Responsibilities and the Communitarian Agenda*. London, Fontana.

Evans, M. (2001) 'Welfare to Work and the Organisation of Opportunity: Lessons from Abroad?', *CASE report 15*. London, Centre for Analysis of Social Exclusion, London School of Economics.

Fasenfest, D., Ciancanelli, P. and Reese, L. A. (1997) 'Value, Exchange and the Social Economy: Framework and Paradigm Shift in Urban Policy', *International Journal of Urban and Regional Research*, 21, 1: 7–22.

Financial Times (1998) 'Pioneer Shows How to Furnish the Market with Jobs', 25 March: 10.

Firn, J. (1975) 'External Control and Regional Development; the Case of Scotland', *Environment and Planning A*, 7: 393–414.

Flores, F. and Gray, J. (2000) *Entrepreneurship and the Wired Life*. London, Demos.

Foster, J. (1999) *Docklands: Cultures in Conflict, Worlds in Collision*. London, University College London Press.

Frances, N. (1988) *Turning Houses into Homes*. London, Fabian Society.

Fuller, D. and Jonas, A. (2002) 'Future Geographies of Financial Inclusion: Changes and Challenges Confronting the British Credit Union Movement', *Antipode*, forthcoming.

Galbraith, J. K. (1992) *The Culture of Contentment*. London, Sinclair-Stevenson.

Geddes, M. (2000) 'Tackling Social Exclusion in the European Union? The Limits to the New Orthodoxy of Local Partnership', *International Journal of Urban and Regional Research*, 24, 4: 782–800.

Giddens, A. (1998) *The Third Way: The Renewal of Social Democracy*. Cambridge, Polity Press.

—— (2000) *The Third Way and its Critics*. Cambridge, Polity Press.

Gittell, R. and Vidal, A. (1998) *Community Organizing: Building Social Capital as a Development Strategy*. London, Sage.

Glennerster, H., Lupton, R., Noden, P. and Power, A. (1999) 'Poverty, Social Exclusion and Neighbourhood: Studying the Area Bases of Social Exclusion', *Case Papers* No. 22, March. London, Centre for the Analysis of Social Exclusion, London School of Economics.

Goetz, E. G. and Clarke, S. E. (eds) (1993) *The New Localism: Comparative Urban Politics in a Global Era*. Newbury Park, CA, Sage.

Gorz, A. (1982) *Farewell to the Working Class*. London, Pluto Press.

—— (1999) *Reclaiming Work*. Cambridge, Polity.

Gough, I. (1979) *The Political Economy of the Welfare State*. London, Macmillan.

Greffe, X. (1998) 'Local Job Development and the Third System', paper presented to the *Third System and Employment Seminar*, held jointly by the European Parliament's Employment and Social Affairs Committee and DG5 of the European Commission, 24–5 September. Published in DG5 (1999) *Third System and Employment Seminar Proceedings*. Brussels, Commission of the European Communities (CEC) (CE-V/1–99–0004–EN-C). Copies available from 200 rue de la Loi, 1049 Brussels.

Grimes, A. (1997) 'Tuning into the Third Sector', *New Economy*, 4, 4 (Winter): 226–9.

Hansenne, M. (1997) 'Statement by Mr Michel Hansenne, Director-General, International Labour Office' at an ILO conference on *Social Policy and Economic Performance*. Amsterdam, 23 January.

Haughton, G. (1998) 'Principles and Practice of Community Economic Development', *Regional Studies: Journal of the Regional Studies Association*, 32, 9, December: 872–7.

—— (ed.) (1999) *Community Economic Development*. London, The Stationery Office.

Hayton, K. (1996) 'A Critical Examination of the Role of Community Business in Urban Regeneration', *Town Planning Review*, 67, 1: 1–19.

—— (2000) 'Scottish Community Business: An Idea that Has Had its Day?', *Policy and Politics*, 28, 2: 193–206.

Hayton, K., Turok, I., Gordon, J. and Gray, J. (1993) *Community Business in Scotland: A Final Report Submitted to Scottish Local Authorities and Scottish Enterprise National*. Glasgow, Centre for Planning, University of Strathclyde.

Hirst, P. Q. (1994) *Associative Democracy: New Forms of Economic and Social Governance*. Cambridge, Polity.

Hoggett, P. (1997) 'Contested Communities', in P. Hoggett (ed.) *Contested Communities: Experiences, Struggles, Policies*. Bristol, Policy Press: 3–16.

House of Commons (2001) *Fifth Report into New Deal and Welfare to Work*. Houses of Parliament, Westminster, Select Committee on Education and Employment. Available from: http://www.parliament.the-stationery-office.co.uk/pa/cm200001/cmselect/cmeduemp/58/5806.htm

Hudson, R. and Williams, A. (1999) 'Re-shaping Europe; the Challenge of New Divisions within a Homogenized Political-Economic Space', in R. Hudson and A. Williams (eds) *Divided Europe: Society and Territory*. London, Sage: 1–28.

Hutton, W. (1996) *The State We're In*, 2nd edn. London, Vintage.

Inman, P. (1999) '35 per cent of New Dealers Leave for "Unknown Destination": Trainees Lured from Scheme by Short-Term Jobs'. *The Guardian*, 13 August: 20.

Jouen, M. (2000) 'European Union Action to Promote Local Employment Initiatives', research paper in the series *European Problems*. Paris, Groupement d'Études et de Recherches Notre Europe. Available from: http://www.notre-europe.asso.fr/Publications-en.htm#Problematiques

Lash, S. (1994) 'Reflexivity and its Doubles: Structure, Aesthetics, Community', in U. Beck, A. Giddens and S. Lash, *Reflexive Modernization: Politics, Tradition and Aesthetics in the Modern Social Order*. Cambridge, Polity Press: 110–73.

Leadbeater, C. (1997) *The Rise of the Social Entrepreneur*. London, Demos.

Lee, R. (1996) 'Moral Money? LETS and the Social Construction of Local Economic Geographies in Southeast England', *Environment and Planning A*, 28, 8 (August): 1377–94.

—— (1999) 'Local Money: Geographies of Autonomy and Resistance?', in R. Martin (ed.) *Money and the Space Economy*. Chichester, John Wiley.

Levitas, R. (1996) 'The Concept of Social Exclusion and the New Durkheimian Hegemony', *Critical Social Policy*, 16, 46: 5–20.

—— (1998) *The Inclusive Society? Social Exclusion and New Labour*. London, Macmillan.

Leyshon, A. and Thrift, N. (1997) *Money/Space*. London, Routledge.

Lionais, D. (2001) 'The Potential for Community-based Economics at Local and Extra-local Scales', Graduate Discussion Paper. Durham, University of Durham, Department of Geography. 33 pp.

Lipietz, A. (1992) *Towards a New Economic Order: Postfordism, Ecology and Democracy*. Oxford, Oxford University Press.

—— (1995) *Green Hopes: The Future of Political Ecology*. Cambridge, Polity Press.

McArthur, A. A. (1993) 'An Exploration of Community Business Failure', *Policy and Politics*, 21, 3: 219–30.

McGregor, A., Clark, S., Ferguson, Z. and Scullion, J. (1997) *Valuing the Social Economy: The Social Economy and Social Inclusion in Lowland Scotland*. Glasgow, Independent Report for Community Enterprise in Strathclyde Ltd, TERU, University of Glasgow, CEiS and Simon Clarke Associates.

Madanipour, A., Cars, G. and Allen, J. (eds) (1998) *Social Exclusion in European Cities: Processes, Experiences and Responses*. London and Philadelphia, PA, Jessica Kingsley Publishers and Regional Studies Association.

Malpass, P. (1994) 'Policy Making and Local Governance: How Bristol Failed to Secure City Challenge Funding (Twice)', *Policy and Politics*, 22, 4: 301–12.

Massey, D. (1991) 'A Global Sense of Place', *Marxism Today*, June: 24–9.

Mollenkopf, J. H. (1983) *The Contested City*. Princeton, NJ, Princeton University Press.

Molloy, A., McFeely, C. and Connolly, E. (1999) *Building a Social Economy for the New Millennium*. Derry, Guildhall Press/NICDA.

Mouffe, C. (2000) *The Democratic Paradox*. London, Verso.

North, P. (1998) 'LETS, "Hours" and the Swiss "Business Ring"', *Local Economy*, 13: 114–32.

Oatley, N. (2000) 'New Labour's Approach to Age-old Problems', *Local Economy*, 15, 2: 86–97.

O'Connor, J. (1973) *The Fiscal Crisis of the State*. London, St Martin's Press.

Offe, C. and Heinze, R. G. (1992) *Beyond Employment: Time, Work and the Informal Economy*. Cambridge, Polity.

Pacione, M. (1995) *Glasgow: The Socio-Spatial Development of the City*. London, Academy Editions.

Pearce, J. (1993) *At the Heart of the Community Economy: Community Enterprise in a Changing World*. London, Calouste Gulbenkian Foundation.

Peck, J. (1998a) 'From Federal Welfare to Local Workfare? Remaking Canada's Work-Welfare Regime', in A. Herod, G. O'Tuathail and S. A. Roberts (eds) *An Unruly World: Globalisation, Governance and Geography*. London, Routledge: 95–115.

—— (1998b) 'New Labourers? Making a New Deal for the "Workless Class"'. Paper presented to the Annual Conference of the Royal Geographical Society/Institute of British Geographers, Guildford, 5–8 January. Mimeo.

Peck, J. and Theodore, N. (1999) 'Insecurity in Work and Welfare: Towards a Trans-Atlantic Model of Labour Regulation?', Paper presented to the Annual Conference of the Royal Geographical Society/Institute of British Geographers, Leicester, 4–7 January.

Pierson, C. (1991) *Beyond the Welfare State: The New Political Economy of Welfare*. Cambridge, Polity.

Power, A. and Bergin, E. (1999) 'Neighbourhood Management', *CASE Papers* No. 31, December. London, Centre for the Analysis of Social Exclusion, London School of Economics.

Procacci, G. (1978) 'Social Economy and the Government of Poverty', *Ideology and Consciousness*, No. 4 (Autumn): 55–72.

——(1999) 'Poor Citizens: Social Citizenship and the Crisis of Welfare States', in S. Hänninen (ed.) *Displacement of Social Policies*. Jyväskylä, SoPhi.

Punter, J. V. (1993) 'Development Interests and the Attack on Planning Controls – Planning Difficulties in Bristol 1985–1990', *Environment and Planning A*, 25, 4: 521–38.

Putnam, R. (1993) *Making Democracy Work*. Princeton, NJ, Princeton University Press.

Rifkin, J. (1995) *The End of Work*. New York, Putnam.

——(1999) 'Work, Social Capital and the Rebirth of Civil Society: A Blueprint for a New Third Sector Politics', Paper given to the Parliamentarians and NGOs Conference, *Market-Oriented Society, Democracy, Citizenship and Solidarity: An Area of Confrontation?* Strasbourg, 31 May–6 June. Available from: http://stars.coe.fr/Dossiers/Societe/ E_JeremyRifkin.htm

——(2000) *The Age of Access*. New York, Tarcher/Putnam.

Rimke, H. (2000) 'Governing Citizens Through Self-help Literature', *Cultural Studies*, 14, 1: 61–78.

Room, G. (ed.) (1995) *Beyond the Threshold: The Measurement and Analysis of Social Exclusion*. Bristol, Policy Press.

Rose, N. (1998) 'The Crisis of the "Social": Beyond the Social Question', in S. Hänninen (ed.): *Displacement of Social Policies*. Jyväskylä, SoPhi.

Saunders, R. (1997) *Resident Services Organisations*. London, Priority Estates Project.

Sennett, R. (1998) *The Corrosion of Character*. New York, WW Norton and Company.

Sewel, J. (1998) *Social Inclusion: Opening the Door to a Better Scotland*. Edinburgh, The Scottish Office.

Silver, H. (1994) 'Social Exclusion and Social Solidarity: Three Paradigms', *International Labour Review*, 133: 531–78.

Smith, D. M. (2000) 'Social Justice Revisited', *Environment and Planning A*, 31: 1149–62.

Smith, G. R. (1999) 'Area-based Initiatives: The Rationale and Options for Area Targeting', *CASE Papers* No. 25, May. London, Centre for the Analysis of Social Exclusion, London School of Economics.

Social Enterprise London (SEL) (2000) *New Directions – Sustaining London's Communities*, London, SEL. Available from: http://www.sel.org.uk

——(2001) *Introducing Social Enterprise*. London, SEL. Available from: http://www.sel.org.uk

Social Exclusion Unit (SEU) (1998) *Bringing Britain Together: A National Strategy for Neighbourhood Renewal*. London, The Stationery Office (cm. 4045).

——(2001) *A New Commitment to Neighbourhood Renewal National Strategy Action Plan*. London, SEU.

Streeck, W., Rogers Hollingsworth, J. and Schmitter, C. (eds) (1994) *Governing Capitalist Economies: Performance and Control of Economic Sectors.* Oxford, Oxford University Press.

Thompson, W., and Hart, F. (1972) *The UCS Work-In.* London, Lawrence and Wishart.

Tilson, B., Mawson, J., Beazley, M., Burfitt, A., Collinge, C., Hall, S., Loftman, P., Nevin, B. and Srbljanin, A. (1997) 'Partnerships for Regeneration: The Single Regeneration Budget Challenge Fund Round One', *Local Government Studies*, 23, 1 (Spring): 1–15.

Turok, I. and Edge, N. (1999) *The Jobs Gap in Britain's Cities: Employment Loss and Labour Market Consequences.* Bristol, Policy Press for the Joseph Rowntree Foundation.

Turok, I. and Webster, D. (1998) 'The New Deal: Jeopardised by the Geography of Unemployment?', *Local Economy*, February.

UNESCO (1999) *Most Clearing House Best Practices for Human Settlements: Social Exclusion/Integration.* Paris, United Nations Educational, Scientific and Cultural Organisation (UNESCO). Available from: http://www.unesco.org/most/bpsocial.htm

Walzer, M. (ed.) (1995) *Towards a Global Civil Society*, Oxford, Berghahn Books.

West, A. (1999) 'Regeneration, Community and the Social Economy', in G. Haughton (ed.) *Community Economic Development.* London, The Stationery Office/Regional Studies Association: 23–9.

Willetts, D. (1999) 'Reviving Civic Conservatism', in A. Kilmarnock (ed.) *The Social Market and the State.* London, Social Market Foundation.

Williams, C. C. and Windebank, J. (1998) *Informal Employment in the Advanced Economies: Implications for Work and Welfare.* London, Routledge.

Wolfensohn, J. (1997) 'The Challenge of Inclusion', Speech to the Annual Meeting of the World Bank, Hong Kong, 23 September. Mimeo. Available from: http://www.worldbank.org/html/extdr/am97/jdw_sp/jwsp97e.htm

Wood, C. and Vamplew, C. (1999) *Neighbourhood Images in Teesside: Regeneration or Decline?* York, Joseph Rowntree Foundation/YPS.

Index

Hayton, K. 63, 124
healthy living centre 111
heterogeneity 29, 121
Hoggett, P. 14, 18
homecare services 33
homeless, services for 99–100
housing associations 1, 110–11
housing estates 45–6, 58, 59, 90, 101–2;
  stigmatisation of 56, 76
housing services 69–70, 74, 102, 107–8

income, from commercial activities 37,
  38–9, 70, 77, 103
industrial economies, decline of 52, 84,
  86
Intermediate Labour Market programmes
  31, 67, 69, 70
intermediation 118
internet services 67
Italy 11

job creation 31–6
job insecurity 4
job search 68
'jobs gap' 53

Keynesian regulation 2

labour market intermediaries 31, 65, 123
labour movement 8
Labour politics (*see also* New Labour) 59
Langridge Initiative Centre
  (Middlesbrough) 77–8, 80
language education 102, 108, 109
Leadbeater, C. 6, 12
leadership 68, 117
learning disabled, services for 48
Lenoir, R. 17
local, and social exclusion 18–20, 22, 29;
  New Labour and 26–8
local associations 8, 121
local community: failures to represent
  45–6; involvement in social economy
  43–4, 76, 80, 103–4, 105, 110–11,
  117; limited management capacity 73,
  77, 79, 80; participation 7–8
local context, importance of 49–50, 80,
  83–91, 119–22
Local Development Companies 65
Local Enterprise Companies 63, 65
local exchange networks 8, 31
Local Initiatives to Combat Social
  Exclusion in Europe (LOCIN) 19, 37
local markets 39–42

local state, role of 60, 72, 79, 80, 81–2,
  94–5, 114, 118, 121; in Bristol 96–7;
  in Glasgow 60, 61, 64–5, 72, 81; in
  Middlesbrough 73, 76–7, 78, 79, 80,
  81; in Tower Hamlets 95–6, 108–9,
  110, 114
localisation 11, 13, 18, 19–20, 26–8,
  41–2, 119
London Docks 87–8
London Docklands Development
  Corporation 88, 95

Maiello, M. 9, 10, 22
mainstream economy, proximity to 41,
  83, 88, 119
management of social enterprises 77;
  professional 68, 69, 77, 99, 103, 105
marginalisation 17
market capacity (*see also* local markets;
  niche markets) 79
market research 68, 118
market social economy 10
mass production 2
Matson Neighbourhood Project
  (Gloucester) 38–9, 43–4, 49
Mediterranean model of social economy
  10–11
Methodists 94
Micklewright, George 97
Middlesbrough 58, 59, 60, 80; economic
  trends 52, 53, 54, 55–6; social
  economy 61, 72–9, 81, 120
Middlesbrough Direct 73
Midwinter, A. 64
minority cultures, presence of 84, 94,
  102–3, 121
modernism 23
Molloy, A. 1, 29
moral economy 23–4
mutuality 7

National Lottery funds 39
*National Strategy for Neighbourhood
  Renewal* 26–7, 28
needs 1, 6, 118, 125
neighbourhoods 27–8
neo-pauperism 6–7
networking 79, 104, 111–12, 115, 118,
  120, 122
New Contract for Welfare 24
New Deal 24–5
New Deal for Communities 27–8, 36, 46
New Labour 11, 22–6; and
  neighbourhood renewal 26–8